Praise for *Living a Life of Greatness*

'A book for the soul. Sarah graciously shares her life to help
you find yours. Sarah's book is a kind reminder that the
best person to care about your life is you. And that
you really can achieve the life you want.'
Liz Hayes

'A brilliant guide to mastering your inner world
and finding true fulfilment and happiness.'
Deepak Chopra

'Sarah Grynberg is a wise and wonderful person, and this
book is a gift that will touch countless lives.'
Johann Hari

'I've never had a conversation with Sarah Grynberg
when I haven't felt I was in the presence of someone
bound for greatness. Her depth and wisdom are
something we should all aspire to.'
Marianne Williamson

SARAH GRYNBERG

Living a Life of Greatness

STEPS TO A FULFILLING EXISTENCE

ALLEN&UNWIN
SYDNEY · MELBOURNE · AUCKLAND · LONDON

First published in 2025

Allen and Unwin
Cammeraygal Country
83 Alexander Street
Crows Nest NSW 2065
Australia
Phone: (61 2) 8425 0100
Email: info@allenandunwin.com
Web: www.allenandunwin.com

Allen and Unwin acknowledges the Traditional Owners of the Country on which we live and work. We pay our respects to all Aboriginal and Torres Strait Islander Elders, past and present.

 A catalogue record for this book is available from the National Library of Australia

ISBN 978 1 76147 083 7

Set in 12/20 pt Minion Pro by Midland Typesetters, Australia
Printed and bound in Australia by the Opus Group

10 9 8 7 6 5 4 3 2 1

The paper in this book is FSC® certified. FSC® promotes environmentally responsible, socially beneficial and economically viable management of the world's forests.

About the author

Sarah Grynberg is a keynote speaker and mindset coach who empowers professional athletes, senior executives and business owners to reach new heights in their personal and professional lives by helping them overcome unhelpful thinking and achieve greatness. With a wealth of experience and a unique approach, Sarah has become the go-to expert in the art of cultivating a powerful mindset.

Sarah's expertise extends to her work as an accomplished writer, focusing on the themes of mindset, mental resilience and happiness. Her insights have helped countless individuals and businesses achieve greatness. She hosts live shows in front of packed audiences, including 2024 a tour across seven states in Australia and New Zealand with renowned author Johann Hari. Sarah is also the creator and host of the internationally acclaimed podcast *A Life of Greatness*, where she has had the privilege of interviewing notable personalities such as

Matthew McConaughey, Andrew Huberman, Geena Davis, Esther Perel, former prime minister John Howard, Deepak Chopra and others. She also has a supplementary podcast series, *Sarah's Greatness*, in which she answers listeners' questions around the power of kindness, finding purpose, habits for achieving greatness, how to stop caring what others think of you and the power of listening.

In addition to her coaching, broadcasting and writing, Sarah has created guided meditations for both children and adults, available through her website.

To my children, Oliver and Poppy: you remind me every day that pure love is precious and to be treasured. May your lives be full of endless possibilities and the same profound joy you bring to my world.

CONTENTS

CONTENTS

Introduction

The path to greatness

What you seek is seeking you.

Rumi

Have you ever had the feeling that something in your life is not quite right? Everything might look good on the outside; you might have ticked all the boxes you thought you wanted to. But inside, something feels empty, or maybe just a little off. Achievements you worked hard for may not feel as life-changing as you had hoped. Unexpected challenges may have led you in directions you didn't plan for. Little by little, despite your careful cultivation, your life path may have strayed from what you really wanted, deep down in your bones. Maybe you feel guilty because you *should* be happy with your successes, and be grateful for what you have, right? But still that feeling something is amiss continues. And, over time, the niggle can become a roar.

I know this feeling well. It came upon me slowly, over a lifetime of a thousand cuts, until one day I realised I had lost myself. I was only surviving, not thriving. It shocked me, but it also gave me a reason to change and reclaim myself and my life. It prompted me to recover my sense of purpose and aliveness. I discovered the essential elements to living a life of greatness, those things that can help fill our days with meaning and our world with joy—and now I want to share them with you, in this book.

Living a life of greatness isn't about building a career, having a fabulous home or even finding work-life balance. Greatness is an interior state of being that is developed through the cultivation of thoughts, practices and values that support you in achieving your full potential. Greatness is synonymous with self-actualisation— the complete realisation of your full potential. Greatness is about living a fulfilling life; it's about knowing and becoming all that you are capable of being. It's building your self-knowledge so that you understand and appreciate who and how you are. It involves mastery of your interior life, rather than your exterior life.

Each of us has a different concept of what greatness means, but there is also a universal understanding that living with a sense of contentment and fulfilment is fundamental to greatness. Greatness is developed deep inside us if we live with a sense of purpose, knowing that our life has meaning. Greatness means we practise self-love. The real goal of greatness, I think, is to live a life of peace and grace.

The path to greatness

With the right information, at the right time, we can create our lives anew. For some people, change is triggered by a major life crisis. I honour the journey of every person who finds themselves on this path; but I also know that, with conscious awareness, we can create real changes in our life without having to hit rock bottom first. We can, with good grace and loving kindness, create the life we seek. And we can start by understanding that it's not our fault if we are a little off track.

Each of us began our life in a state of greatness, in a place of unlimited possibility and potential. Babies and young children view the world with awe and wonder. Deep inside us we understand who we are and what we are here to do. But life intervenes. Our experiences affect us. We suffer loss; we learn to survive. We live in a system with many expectations. Every day we learn how to adapt to the social and emotional conditioning that is part of our society. We learn the rules for being a 'good' citizen. We also learn that there are parts of us we need to downplay, or even lose, if we are to be acceptable. Little by little we splinter away some of our essence. Little by little we dilute the greatness—the essential, wondrous sense of fulfilment—that we are born with.

It might sound radical, but the idea that we can return home to our innate truth is at the heart of life. The ultimate and most beautiful homecoming awaits you. I know this because I have been there.

Not so long ago, I was living my dream life. I was a producer in breakfast radio, and from the outside my life looked perfect. Even I believed the facade. I am an achievement-orientated person and through hard work and dedication I had climbed the ladder of success and become a producer on one of the biggest radio shows in Australia. The program I worked on was a household name, with some well-known Australian talent. I attended amazing media events and spent my days in a dynamic and demanding environment where I was rubbing shoulders with all sorts of media personalities. I felt supremely lucky to have such a great job, and I presented to the world with a happy and vivacious exterior. I did love my job—but deep down I felt miserable. This left me in a perpetual state of confusion. How could I feel so sad when everything looked to be going my way?

What the world couldn't see was that over time my life had slowly become more and more unbalanced. Work, and the idea of success that came with it, was my whole world. My alarm went off at 3.30 a.m. I was out the front door before my family even stirred, because that was the way breakfast radio worked. I drove my car through darkened streets well before dawn to get to the office and start my day before the rest of the world had even woken. After a long day at work, I picked up my young children from creche and kinder and headed home to feed and bathe them and complete all the other life tasks our family needed. Then I fell into an exhausted heap, going to bed before my husband even got home from work. I did this week in, week out. I lived in a haze, often not knowing if it was day or night. My mind felt constantly jetlagged, and my body was starting to crash. Exhaustion took over. I was so tired I couldn't sleep. My mind whirred with worries that I would sleep through my alarm, and my body felt constantly wired. When I did eventually fall asleep, my rest was fitful and failed to refresh me. Then, the next morning, I struggled to force myself to get up again. It was a constant cycle, and clearly I was not coping. But I kept going, kept pushing myself, because I had a great job and a fabulous life.

I tried to implement coping mechanisms, but fifteen-minute power naps in the afternoon seemed to make things worse, and meditation had little effect on my cortisol-infused mind. I was in a permanent state of survival mode and constantly 'on call'. For the first time, a niggly little voice inside had me questioning myself. *Is this really the right job for me?* But I kept on going. I felt sorrow and guilt that I was missing out on so much time with my children and my husband. I had moments of frustration, and I was easily irritated. I forgot important events. I knew I was sacrificing my life with my family for my career, but I was subsumed in the chaos and I couldn't back down. On reflection, I became a bit of a martyr. I downplayed my feelings at work for months. I chided myself for having such a lack of gratitude. My health started to suffer. But still, I put on a brave face and pretended everything was okay. I was a terrific study in keeping it together and handling everything that came my way.

Then, one cold winter morning, the life I had consciously crafted to within an inch of perfection suddenly came to a standstill. When my alarm went off, I could barely lift my cheek from the pillow. My head felt stuffy and my nose had started to run. My chest felt congested and I had an uncontrollable coughing fit that wracked my lungs. Every muscle in my body was aching; I felt hot one minute and cold the next. The flu had finally caught up with me. I mustered the energy to get dressed but I was so lightheaded I had to be real with myself. Today was not the day to go to work. I reluctantly texted my boss to tell him I couldn't come in, then crawled back under the warm blankets and fell back to sleep. I couldn't remember the last time I'd had a sick day.

A few hours later I emerged from the cocoon of restless slumber and started planning how I could get back to work the next day. A honey and lemon drink felt like a good start, so I stood up to make my way to the kitchen. A wave of dizziness came over me. I dropped to my hands and knees, crawling my way to the pantry. I held on to the bench as the kettle boiled and willed myself to get better. I was, in my usual way, going to overcome this by sheer strength. But another wave of dizziness washed over me, and I began to feel sorry for myself. I started to wonder how my life had become so empty. If I couldn't work, what was my existence worth? I felt bereft and alone.

I suddenly realised my dream job had turned me into a fraction of myself.

Outside the window, the world looked bleak. The tree branches were empty and stark against the grey winter sky. I felt the same inside. I tried to tell myself I was just sick and it would be okay, but then a tiny sparrow appeared and hopped jubilantly from branch to branch directly outside the kitchen window. I envied that bird. My eyes welled up with tears and then, without warning, I started to sob uncontrollably. Huge wet tears rolled down my face. I coughed, I cried, I spluttered. I was a complete mess. I couldn't stop it. Every part of me that had resisted this moment for years finally lost the battle. I realised how far I had veered from my heart. I had hit rock bottom.

I reached for another tissue as the realisations kept coming. I was more than simply tired. I was under a heavy dark cloud that made it hard to breathe. My life felt empty. Looking back, I think I was experiencing a type of existential crisis, what Eckhart Tolle and many others call 'the dark night of the soul'.

I willed myself to regain some semblance of control. I blew my nose again and tried to still the swirl of emotion inside me. Deep down I knew I was pleading for a life change, but it scared me—there would be no turning back. I had fought so hard for my dream, for my idea of a perfect life. Who would I be without this identity? I felt trapped. I knew I couldn't recover from this exhaustion by doing the same thing that created it. And I knew with my whole being that if I continued on this road of next-to-nil self-care and zero quality time with my family I would only compound my misery. I was as far from myself as I had ever been. The sense that my heart was completely incongruent with my body was palpable. This sickness was a desperate cry for help from my own body, amplified by my heart.

I knew I was experiencing burnout, a chronic stress condition that builds over time, resulting in exhaustion, disengagement and a lack of work-life balance. I felt the truth of this self-diagnosis in my bones. Naming what I was feeling helped me make sense of the emotional waves that had consumed me. I decided I needed to free myself from my current reality, and do something, anything, to move forward. But it was up to me—no one else could do it for me.

This singular, defining experience could be called many different things: a lightbulb moment, a spiritual awakening, a moment of truth, a blind flash of the obvious. But even though my conscience had made a choice, and there was a voice in my head clearly telling me I had to make a change, I felt resistance. I second-guessed myself, telling the voice that I would 'see how I went' once I was well again. A few days later, I set the alarm for 3.30 a.m. and returned to work. In fear of the unknown, I chose to remain superglued to my job—*just for a bit longer*, I bargained. I thought it was better for me, at that time, to remain in something I knew well, even though my emotional, mental and physical wellbeing were trash. I chose predictability and safety over uncertainty.

And then, a few weeks later, an utter stranger crossed my path. Buddhist monks say, 'When the student is ready, the teacher will come.' That is what happened to me.

I was waiting in line for a coffee at my local when a deep voice behind me spoke.

'I see you're reading *The Power of Now.*'

When I turned around, I found a tall man with longish dark-brown hair and an open, clean-shaven face. He was right: tucked under my arm was one of the first personal development books I had ever read—recommended to me by a friend after I'd confessed to her I had been feeling a little lost.

'Eckhart Tolle is one of my favourite mindfulness teachers. His teachings had such a profound effect on my life,' the man continued, without pausing.

I nodded, unsure what to say.

'I'm Tom,' he added with his hand stretched out.

'Sarah,' I replied as the barista popped lids on both our coffees at the same time. I was immediately and instinctively curious about Tom, something I hadn't felt for a little while.

We moved outside to a table in the sunshine, where we chatted easily about the book and our lives. When I looked at my watch, I couldn't believe an hour had already passed.

Tom was easily one of the most fascinating people I had ever spoken with. He told me how he had wanted to be a Buddhist monk, and had lived in an ashram for years, spending long days deep in meditation. He had devoted weeks to silence and trained both his mind and his body in many traditions of religion and spirituality.

'I don't subscribe to a particular belief system. I consider myself to be a lover of all, as they have all played a part in shaping my views of the world,' he offered, and the truth of this landed in my heart. There was so much I wanted to ask him; so much that in my haze of work burnout I'd never taken the time to think about.

Tom and I met every week for months. We talked about human behaviour, psychology and the mind-body connection, and he opened my eyes to many different personal development approaches and traditions. He gave me a reading list and I studied all the books he recommended. I embodied all I was learning every day in my life.

And an incredible thing happened. The more deeply I immersed myself in these learnings, the more I started to see my life change. I continued to struggle with work-life balance immensely, because I still felt I had to keep going. But there were tiny glimmers of hope within the demands of my life, as I parented my young children and navigated a hardcore job that required me to be 'on' constantly. I found myself making small changes that made me feel optimistic. I was able to look at my life through a lens that was more forgiving, loving and empathetic. Something was slowly unlocking. Life was starting to bubble back up inside me, washing away the sadness and despair I had considered my normal. They were tiny steps, but I had started somewhere. I had a sense of possibility.

Then life decided to intervene . . . again.

Hi Sarah, we need to meet in person tomorrow, announced the text. I thought it was odd that my boss was flying down to Melbourne from Sydney to see me, and it made me a little nervous. A weird feeling of dread lingered in my stomach as I entered the meeting room the next day.

'Sarah', he said, 'the show's production is going through a restructure, and your role will be moving to Sydney. Would you be interested in relocating?'

Caught off guard, I didn't know what to say. I had a family with two young children, my husband had a job he loved, and all my friends and family were here in Melbourne.

'Hmm', I said slowly. 'I don't think that's possible for me.'

As I sat there across from him, I started feeling concerned about my future. *What will I do with no job?* I thought about the seven years I'd been working for this company. *What am I supposed to do next?*

But after months of immersing myself in philosophical and spiritual teachings, something inside me was different. Instead of going into full-blown panic mode, an inner knowing swept over me. I was embodying all the teachings I was learning, and wisdom was starting to filter in. I was more aware of myself: of how I was showing up in the world, and the power of my words and thought patterns. Even though I was terrified, I felt a hint of protection. I was not devastated by this news; it would be okay.

That night, as I lay in bed and reflected on my day, I started to tear up. I found words forming inside my head. I was not a religious person, but nevertheless I found myself talking to someone.

I am feeling lost and scared, and I don't know where I am headed next, I thought. *What I really want to do now is something more, something that is going to make a difference in this world.*

I wanted to work in an environment full of love, where I had a sense of purpose that was greater than myself. I wanted work that would not only fulfil me, but others too. I wanted to work more practical hours in a job that didn't impact so heavily on my health, or my family.

I uttered these words—perhaps you might call them prayers—and fell into a deep sleep. I had spoken my truth, but I had no idea who was listening or if my desires would ever be answered. I simply felt a willingness to receive life.

Two weeks later, I received a call from Dave, an executive at the radio station I worked for.

'We heard the news about the relocation of your job, and we don't want to see you go. We see your value and believe in your talent and skills. Would you be interested in being part of our podcasting team?'

I was a little unsure what podcasting actually involved because, at the time, the medium was still in its infancy. However, I had listened to *Serial,* and I had enjoyed it. So, in shock, I muttered, 'Umm, yes.'

Dave went on to tell me in confidence, 'Hamish and Andy are about to finish up their radio show and start a podcast. We really want you to be their executive producer. There would be no break-fast hours to juggle. You would work normal business hours.'

In that moment, all my prayers had been actioned—and in a way that was far greater than I could ever have dreamed of. It felt like a miracle.

I started the new role in a team that was vibrant and full of love. I was learning so much and had an amazing boss who saw the light in me. And, most of all, I was able to restore a sense of balance in my life. My strength and wellbeing returned.

I continued to research human behaviour and what created happiness. I explored why some people who had everything were deeply miserable, while others with very little were tremendously happy. I learned about how knowing our true values and belief systems helped us to make the right choices for ourselves and live life in a happier and more conscious way. But deep down I knew that I was still *responding* to my life, making changes only when I was placed in a position where I had to.

A couple of months later, I had a flash of inspiration during a meditation. The idea for my *A Life of Greatness* podcast, a platform through which I could serve others, was born. My studies had led me to the idea of greatness and what a life of greatness can look like. I wanted to hold meaningful conversations with global thought leaders who would generously share their way of thinking with my audience.

This felt like a considered and aligned choice for change. It was something I had moved towards with each step I had made. I wouldn't have been able to take action if I had not invested so much of myself into getting the basics right in my life. None of it would have happened if I hadn't made the conscious decision to shift my life towards greatness. I would have kept on doing the same thing, waiting for something to happen to break me out of my miserable spell.

When I told my boss about my idea for the podcast, and he said he would back it, I dived in with a rush of energy and urgency. As I started interviews for my first season, I was overjoyed by the meaningful conversations I was having with so many wise people. I knew in my gut that this podcast was going to be a success, and my instincts were confirmed. The numbers spoke for themselves—but, more importantly, so did the audience response. I was overwhelmed by the messages I was getting from total strangers who had been moved by the episodes. It felt as if what I had asked for in my prayers that night had been heard and deeply honoured.

The path to greatness

Many of us dread making changes in our lives because we are attached to what we know. We are conditioned to avoid fear, and we don't typically look more deeply to understand what our existence is truly about. Life-altering choices require us to risk leaving our comfort zones, yet leaving our old selves behind can mean discovering who we truly are.

And this just happens to be the most exciting part.

Every day, I hear stories from global leaders, celebrities and entrepreneurs about disappointment, unexpected outcomes and even failures they have experienced, only to transform their lives by actioning change and gaining virtues of wisdom and strength as an essential part of their growth. I recognise there are many people who are happy in their lives who don't seek to change the status quo, but for others, feelings of discontent or misery, once acknowledged, can be an amazing catalyst for change. Greatness can come from rebuilding ourselves, rather than remaining stuck in who we have unwittingly become. These types of life changes can only be actioned by you, and through you. You alone have the power to rewrite your own story in alignment with your truest self.

When you make a clear decision to take control of your life and move closer to your truth—to who you are and what you really want—something truly remarkable happens: life starts moving in a more fulfilling direction. When you stand in your truth, the world will open up for you. You get to redesign your future on your own terms.

The journey towards greatness may not be smooth. There will be challenges and setbacks along the way. I had to be pushed to my limits before I was redirected towards a life of meaning and fulfilment. There are many roads to navigate and unexpected detours to take, but you are always free to move in the direction that matters.

If you feel you have lost your way, this book will teach you how to regain your inner light. Each chapter will give you the tools and wisdom you need to bring yourself back 'home'. You will discover who you truly are and gain clarity about the life you deserve to live. You will explore the value of breath and meditation in daily life; you will discover the power of purpose; and you will take time to reflect on how intention, forgiveness, love and trusting your own instincts are keys to living a life of greatness. Every chapter has its own gift to share.

A life aligned with your true nature looks different for everyone, but there are common elements everyone can master. That's all part of the uniqueness of the human experience.

Welcome to the first steps on your right path—your path to realising your fullest potential. May these words fill you with wisdom and knowledge, guiding you to a life of greatness.

Chapter 1

The stories you tell yourself

There is nothing either good or bad but thinking makes it so.

William Shakespare, *Hamlet*

When I first read Endi's text, I laughed out loud. Endi and I had been friends for a few years, and she knew as well as anyone my feelings about cold weather. I was not a fan. I read her text sitting up in my cosy bed, with the electric blanket on high and an extra rug across my lap.

'Hey,' I said to my husband. 'Can I read you something funny?'

He nodded and put his book down.

'Endi is inviting me to go on a retreat with her next month,' I told him. 'But the catch is, it's one of those Wim Hof retreats with ice bathing.'

'That sounds great. You should go,' he said without a moment of hesitation.

'But I hate the cold,' I said.

'That's exactly why you should go,' he replied.

You might think that being born in June would have set me up to have some type of affinity with the cold. That I would relish the thick coats and warm woollen socks that keep us toasty during the cold months. I don't. The cold creeps into my bones every season of the year. I fuss about achieving the perfect temperature of 23 degrees in my home, my car and my office. While others wander around in weather-appropriate clothing, I am in multiple layers ready to ward off the slightest hint of chill. This has been my relationship with the cold since I was a child, and even with my best intentions it has remained true to this day.

I think I was born with a fear of the cold. There was no inciting event where I got lost in the snow; I just remember always being cold-phobic. The discomfort I felt in my body and the lack of control I had over my trembling made me want to avoid feeling cold at all costs. My internal thermostat seemed different to everyone else's, and this alone made me feel like the odd one out. I imagined I might grow out of my fear of the cold, but it persisted. During my university days, I lived with a small heater blasting my feet while I studied because I couldn't concentrate otherwise. When I felt cold I couldn't be present, let alone focus.

Wim Hof, on the other hand, embraces the cold. He earned the nickname 'The Iceman' by breaking world records related to cold exposure. The extreme athlete ran an Arctic Circle half marathon barefoot, endured standing in a container of ice cubes for more than 112 minutes and wore shorts when he climbed Mount Kilimanjaro. His ability to withstand extreme temperatures was developed during years of training to control his breathing, heart rate and blood circulation. I shivered just thinking about it.

Endi's invitation was to join her at a weekend retreat where we would participate in cold-exposure activities, including an ice bath, with the aim of releasing toxins, strengthening the immune system and relieving stress. For me, it would mean facing my serious cold phobia head-on.

I've booked my ticket already. Here's the link so you can get yours, Endi texted. I loved my friend's willingness to try new things. She always had a positive take on life, facing the world with fearlessness and embracing the challenges that came her way. She had captured my attention, but there was still a well-rooted story running in my head.

'No, no, no, I just couldn't do it,' I said to my husband as he turned another page in his book. My mind was racing with questions, fast and furious. *Why would I put myself into a crazy situation where I'd have to face one of the things I most dreaded in life? Why would I spend money on a retreat that I was not going to enjoy, and spend weeks fearing in the lead-up?* I voiced these worries to him.

'As I said before, that's exactly why you should do it,' he said gently. 'Why not see it as an opportunity to step outside your comfort zone? Maybe it's time to change the negative story about cold being something to avoid at all costs that you keep playing on repeat in your mind.'

'What if something happens to me?' I said. 'What if I get so cold, I go into cardiac arrest?' I searched for reasons to say no, to keep my old story alive. My body knew the cold was dangerous—even fatal for humans—and I had read many stories about people dying from cold exposure. I would do anything to avoid the discomfort of the cold.

My husband laughed. 'That won't happen. You will be fine.'

And it was those four words—*you will be fine*—that sparked something in me. My husband was right. What's the worst thing that could happen? I was a fit and healthy person. The idea that I could die slowly and painfully from freezing to death, or that being cold would at the very least make me sick with the flu, was just a negative narrative in my head. Perhaps I could challenge my cold phobia once and for all? I picked up my phone and quickly wrote a text to Endi. *Okay, shitting myself, but in. Will book ticket before I talk myself out of it.* Then I pressed my shaking fingertip on the purchase link, and with that I committed to a two-day Wim Hof retreat. I was going to come face-to-face with my deepest, darkest fear: the cold.

•

The stories you tell yourself

The negative stories we tell ourselves have the power to place limitations on our lives and experiences. They keep us trapped in our comfort zone. Often they're birthed from the limiting self-belief that we are not enough. They can stop us from attempting something new or taking a risk, from leaving relationships, and from making life transitions and changes—leaving a job or relocating to a new state. For some people, thinking about change ignites a positive internal narrative of excitement, action and power. For others, our negative stories can make us feel incapable of change. They can paralyse us in inaction or helplessness, clouding our thoughts and holding us in behaviour loops that prevent us from embracing the full human experience. Challenging the stories we tell ourselves—and realising we are enough and capable of change—is critical in building a life path that is truly our own calling.

When we're given the chance to review the stories we tell ourselves, this is a golden opportunity. If we're open to it, life can prompt us to look at things differently and change how we perceive our experiences. There is freedom in jumping over the hurdle and transforming the stories that keep us from living in our own greatness.

In the days leading up to the retreat, I started to feel uneasy in the pit of my stomach. The incessant chatter of my story had started in my head again. *Why are you putting yourself in a situation that's so uncomfortable? What are the pros to going? You don't have to go if you don't want to.* But I pushed on. I had promised Endi I would go, and I was a person of my word.

The day arrived and Endi came to pick me up. The retreat was an hour's drive away, and even though I am hopeless with directions I tried to navigate. I needed to distract myself from the rising fear of being cold. Still, I wanted to cry.

It was late on a Friday afternoon, and only 7 degrees Celsius. Outside, the world was frosty and overcast. I had dressed hardcore, wearing jeans, a T-shirt, a thick black hoodie and a puffer jacket. The retreat was far from luxurious—more school-camp style with dormitories and bunk beds—but Endi and I were allocated a twin room and I was grateful that I didn't need to share with six strangers. We unpacked our few belongings and I checked for an electric blanket on the bed. No luck there, but fortunately I had come prepared with my hot water bottle and thermals.

Endi and I made our way to the welcome session in the main hall. We sat nervously on yoga mats with 34 other strangers, mostly men, and waited for Sam, the certified Wim Hof instructor, to begin.

'Why have you come to this retreat?' he asked the group.

As we went around the circle, I noticed everyone had a story, a narrative they told the world. I thought about how these stories we tell become habits: ideas about ourselves that we retell again and again without much thought. We believe them and we hold on to them, as they define our lives and who we are. The group had so many different stories to tell. Millie, a high-level corporate executive, had the telltale signs of insomnia etched on her face. George limped into the room, breathing heavily as he sank into a chair. Alan and Jo came in apprehensively with their arms hooked together but a gulf between them. Yet there was a unity between us. We had just come out of two years of harsh Covid-19 lockdowns, and we were all feeling battered and mentally exhausted. One woman's hands shook as she tried to pour a drink of water. Her Parkinson's was progressing faster than she could manage. Evie took extra time to sit comfortably, her joints jammed with arthritis. There were people from all walks of life—plumbers, teachers, ex-military workers and entrepreneurs. We all had goals in common: to overcome the stories in our heads, to conquer our fear of the cold and to seek solace in its healing abilities.

Sam took us through how the retreat would run. There would be two ice baths over the weekend: one for three minutes, and one for five minutes. My story, that I was the coldest person I knew, was about to be tested. That night I fell asleep full of trepidation, but also curiosity.

•

Negative narratives are typically created in childhood—perhaps in response to a single event or, like my fear of the cold, as a slowly developing instinctual aversion. Either way, our narrative dictates our choices, even if we're not conscious of it. We formulate our story as a way to help make sense of the world. By the time we enter adolescence, we already have an internal tale about who we are and what the world is like. This narrative runs quietly in the background. It colours the lens through which we perceive and interpret our day-to-day experiences, and it affects our actions and decisions.

Most of what we learn about ourselves is implanted by the time we are seven years old. The experiences we have in our life, even before we have finished primary school, can affect us forever in tangible ways. We write our narrative without the benefits of the life experience we accumulate as adults, without the education we invest in, without all the learning we do through interactions with others: romantic partners, family members, friends. We formulate a set of rules and beliefs about ourselves and the world well before our brains, hearts and minds develop to maturity. No wonder we get stuck in our story loops.

It is an act of immense faith in yourself, and a huge step towards having greater direction in your life, to stop and examine your thinking patterns. You'll know the narratives that are not serving you because you'll feel their crushing weight. Our limiting self-talk—typically rooted in not feeling we are 'enough'—can trick us into believing stories that aren't true. Every time you find yourself doubting your ability—telling yourself you can't do something, without even consciously thinking about it—this is a chance for you to rewrite your story. The giveaway lines for a negative default are usually easy to spot, if you tune in. The voice you hear might sound like an inner critic, bad cop or even a parent or previous teacher. Keep your ears tuned for negative reflex expressions such as, 'I'm not good enough to do this,' 'I always mess things up,' or 'It will never work out.' This is the language of limitation.

'I hate the cold' was a negative narrative that shaped many decisions in my life. I chose not to go on ski holidays with friends, I said no to activities outside during winter and I frequently checked room temperatures to make sure they were warm enough for me. My story about the cold distorted my perspective and created a negative point of view that did not serve my wellbeing. Our negative narratives can take many forms. Perhaps you can relate to a fear of public speaking that stops you putting yourself forward for the job of your dreams, or a personal narrative that says doing things alone means you have no friends or won't be safe, so you never plan that solo holiday to a unique destination.

As adults we can challenge our negative thinking patterns by asking what evidence there is to support them. When you discover the evidence is lacking—and you will—you can consciously change the script about what you believe. It's about flipping the narrative from negative to positive, from inadequacy to adequacy. It's not always easy—you created your stories to protect you from feeling distress and discomfort. They are effectively safety devices you have constructed to provide psychological and physical distance from feeling unease. So be prepared for them to hang on, and be ready for the challenge. 'Everything is possible' and 'I can change what doesn't serve me' may be the first beliefs you try to integrate. Imagine how life would be different if you reframed 'I can't' to 'I can'.

We are the sum of our experiences. Our best insights into who we are today will come from examining the stories that originated in our past. There are many thought leaders who say that all our emotional and personal problems come from us believing we are not enough. But this does not mean we are locked into believing this for the rest of our lives. The human brain is a wonderfully adaptive organ that is capable of immense change. We can give our brain different messages about who we are, and it will listen and take us towards new beliefs.

If you don't know where to start, one of the most powerful stories you can rewrite is the one that says, 'I am not enough.' So many of our negative stories are rooted in childhood experiences during which we decided we are inadequate. You may have grown up without continual praise or loving connections. Even if you did have adequate support, we all exist in a world where we're faced with a constant barrage telling us that we are lacking. So it is no surprise that, for many of us, our front-of-mind story is based on our perceived shortcomings.

There's good news, though: this is an acquired belief, and we can change it.

•

The second day of the retreat was one of preparation. We practised some breathing techniques and learnt about the theory behind the ice bath experience. We discovered that cold water exposure can reduce cortisol release and the way we perceive stress. It also improves cardiovascular function, stimulates circulation, activates the immune system and reduces inflammation in the body.

All around me people shared their stories. I started to enjoy myself as I learned about their reasons for coming and what they wanted to change. Many people spoke of the lingering effects of isolation in the post-Covid world and its impact on their mental health. They shared their worries for their children as they tried to re-enter social circles, and the pressure of making up on lost learning time. I was comforted to know I wasn't the only one who was still trying to recover from the effects of lock-downs. I also wasn't alone in my fear of the cold. I wasn't the only one who harboured a deep-down association between feeling cold and not being able to control my body, who found it unbearably uncomfortable. People wanted to rewrite the stories that bound them. They spoke of releasing past traumas and finally letting go of the negative stories and beliefs they had held on to for so long. They wanted to create new ways to be, to feel alive again, to challenge themselves to live a different story.

Then it was time to get changed for the main event: the dreaded ice bath.

'I'm nervous,' I said to Endi.

'I am too, but it's okay. We will be alright,' she replied.

We rummaged through our suitcases for our bathers.

'God help me, I only have a bikini,' I said.

'Me too,' said Endi, laughing tensely.

It was already dark at 7 p.m., and only 3 degrees outside. It was raining softly when Sam began the session.

'Alright,' Sam said, 'this is how it's going to go. There are four ice baths. Each of them has been freshly filled with ice so they are the right level of coldness.'

The right level of coldness? I thought. *You mean, it needs to be a particular level of cold?* Just thinking about different levels of cold made me feel anxious. Cold was cold, right?

Sam continued. 'We are going to take it in turns. Everyone will need to stand outside as we wait for each round of people to go in. While we are waiting, there is no talking. Everyone needs to do the horse stance.'

The horse stance is a technique Wim Hof designed to help people prepare for cold exposure. It helps develop body strength, muscle tone, stability, balance and endurance. Sam had demonstrated the stance by standing up straight with his feet spread apart, about one-and-a-half times shoulder width. He explained our posture should be upright and aligned with a straight spine. The knees are then bent in a squat, as if we were on horseback. There are also arm movements and deep breathing to focus on while in the pose. We pushed our right hands away from the body to the left side, then did the opposite, making 'hoo-hah' sounds as we went. Sam explained that regular practice of this stance would improve our fitness and the way we felt and moved, and that it is a great way to warm up your body after an ice bath.

'Are you ready?' Sam said. 'Let's do this.'

It was freezing cold and my bikini was already soaked with rain. I was beyond nervous, and cold, and I wasn't even in the ice bath yet. I tried to focus. I did the horse stance, but the negative voice in my head persevered: *I hate this. I can't do this.* A cellist was playing beautiful music and I tried to focus on the notes of his song to take me into a meditative state. The melody was soothing, a distraction before the big event, and it helped. In groups of four, people began the process as Sam talked them through and kept time. Then it was Endi's turn.

'You got this,' I said to her. But as she got into the ice bath, I could see the look of dread on her face. From the sideline I urged her on. She practised the breathing exercise and soon we were counting her down. She had done it.

The next group took their places in the ice baths. One woman lasted only 30 seconds before she started to cry and got out. She sobbed in her friend's arms.

It was almost my turn. *I'm not going to do this*, I thought to myself. I was shaking like crazy. My body felt vulnerable. Freezing to death was a real thing. *What if I have a heart attack? Or get hypothermia and need to be rushed to hospital? Nope, this is not for me*, I thought.

'I don't want to do this either. I just came to support my wife,' said a middle-aged man standing close by. 'It's my first time, too. Why don't you and I do it together?'

The feelings of dread started to drift away as I looked at him and smiled. Here was a stranger, someone I had never even spoken to, and yet he had seen me. His comfort was a catalyst, but more than that: I felt a subtle shift in my mindset. His words were actually helping to change the negative narrative running in my head. I *could* do this. Then I heard more strangers behind me, saying, 'We will be here for you.'

Okay Sarah, I said to myself. *You really can do this.*

I put one leg over the edge of the bath and slid it slowly into the icy water. Then I gradually lowered my other leg into the depths. I crouched down into a squat as the freezing-cold ice cubes rattled against the side of the tub and pressed up against my skin.

'Concentrate on your breath,' I said quietly to myself.

I submerged my body fully and closed my eyes. I was cold inside and out. I asked myself again why I was doing this and, as I got accustomed to the cold, an answer came.

When I started my podcast six years ago, I made a commitment to fully embody the lessons I was speaking about. I wanted to live the positive narrative of greatness that I was teaching others to live by. I wanted to express my full potential. I wanted to be brave and face my fears. I wanted to show up and follow my purpose. I wanted to reframe the negative stories I had told myself so I could embrace new experiences. I realised that when I changed my story, I was not only being true to myself but also enriching others' lives. Submerged in the ice bath I could feel, in that moment, the power and beauty in helping others to break through the stories that bind.

As I acknowledged this, I also realised something else: I had underestimated myself completely. I was resilient. I had great mental strength from my years of self-enquiry and meditation. I was, right there and then, dispelling layers of fear and anxiety, facing what I dreaded most in my life. I was not that story anymore.

Minutes passed as these insights flooded my mind. The cello's notes hummed softly in the background, and I kept my eyes closed.

'Ten more seconds,' announced Sam.

The group started the countdown. My skin was burning: *ten, nine, eight, seven.*

The coldness had seeped into every pore of my body: *six, five, four.*

The last seconds of my ice bath ticked away. I took a deep breath: *three, two, one.*

'That's it!' the group cheered.

I had done it. I fist-pumped the air and stood up.

'You have a strong mind, Sarah. You did very well,' said Sam.

I scrambled out of the ice bath. I couldn't believe it. I felt elated.

'We did it!' I said excitedly as Endi and I hugged. I wrapped myself in a towel, but there was a different kind of warmth spreading through my body. I felt the reality of a new story unfolding in me, one that would help me flourish instead of fear. There was nothing I couldn't do.

That weekend, many people realised how lost they had become in their fear-based stories. We rediscovered the personal super-power of embracing a new narrative—of simply saying, 'I can.' The experience taught me that everyone has a negative narrative in their head—even people who we think have it all together. Academy Award–winning actor Geena Davis talked about this when we chatted on my podcast. The story that kept Geena stuck in her comfort zone was that she never wanted to be a fuss to anyone. Women were to be seen, not heard. She found it hard to speak up until she met actor Susan Sarandon on the set of *Thelma & Louise.* Susan helped Geena realise it was okay for women to voice their opinions and, when they did, they deserved to be listened to. The influence of this friendship changed Geena's life forever: it helped her rewrite the limiting narrative that was driving her life story.

Challenging our narrative can help us become the person we aspire to be.

•

When I spoke with clinician, researcher and mental health and neuroscience teacher Dr Bruce Perry on my podcast, he said that one of the most important factors in growing as adults is to realise our adequacy. As we mature, we should aim to develop a realistic understanding of what life is really like, and acknowledge that no one, not even the person we see as having many gifts, has it perfectly together. When we let go of the endless comparisons that so often dominate our lives, we grant ourselves a sense that we are okay, just as we are. This has a powerful influence on how we think and feel. 'I am enough' is a powerful narrative that, when embraced, will help you challenge the other stories you are running. 'I am enough' is how you can restore your authentic sense of self. It is worth returning to this statement—'I am enough'—again and again, whenever you feel a sense of lack. Keep reminding yourself of it. It will make a difference.

The take-home message here is that your life is yours and yours alone to create. Your story can restart now with a new page where your deepest desires and wildest dreams can take shape. You can author a life of greatness, or you can stay in your comfort zone and keep going back over the same storyline.

This is your invitation to rewrite your story. Make it grand.

Chapter 2

Living with conscious awareness

No problem can be solved from the same level of consciousness that created it.

Unknown

My neck had stiffened from dozing in the chair in Poppy's room. I rubbed it with my right hand and dropped my ear to my shoulder like I had been taught in yoga class. It helped a little. It was still dark and I wasn't even sure what time it was. It must have been super early as the birds were still quiet. For a moment, I felt the stillness of the house and didn't think about the last 24 hours. And then I remembered. My heart immediately beat faster than it should; my skin prickled with heat and my mouth felt dry. Then I started to feel the prickle of annoyance descend on me. I'd worked so hard during the previous few years to respond differently to stress. But sometimes, when tough things happened,

I fell back into my old ways. *I am a work in progress,* I reminded myself. *I am doing the best I can.* Truly, that is all we can ever do.

The blankets started to shift and I watched my two-year-old daughter roll onto her side, still deep in slumber. Dear Poppy, my second-born, my tiny treasure. She looked so vulnerable. I felt tears well up in my eyes again. I struggled to process it all. My mind was blurry with lack of sleep due to hours of worry and worst-case-scenario planning. I knew it was how I was wired, part of my DNA, but I also knew how much I needed to change the way I responded.

Yesterday Poppy was unstoppable—full of energy and mischief, demanding a chocolate milkshake for breakfast and beating her little fists on the kitchen table when I calmly said no.

'But I want some now, Mummy,' she had demanded. I offered her water in her favourite cup, but it wouldn't do. Her face had crumpled in a scowl. She pushed the cup and it spilled, pooling water across the table. I was just holding it together as I reached for some paper towels to soak up the mess. Then Poppy got down off the chair and ran out of the kitchen. She was only out of sight for a few seconds. I was consumed with cleaning when I heard a terrifying thump and then nothing. It was quiet—too quiet. I quickly strode towards the doorway. I can't quite remember the next few minutes, but I know I screamed.

My little blonde-haired girl was lying motionless on the carpet, her face smeared with her own blood. Our coffee table, a solid round hardwood structure that takes two people to lift, was slightly off centre. I knelt at my daughter's side and felt the impact hanging in the air. There was a huge gash above her left eyebrow. She had knocked herself out. I held the wet paper towel I still had in my hand to her forehead to try to stem the bleeding. I was worried it wasn't hygienic enough, but I was more worried about her injury. *Is she concussed? What should I do next? Should I move her? Has she fractured her skull?* I thought the absolute worst as she came to.

At the hospital, I was frightened. When the doctor said they couldn't stitch her up because she needed plastic surgery, I was an untold mess. I watched them roll her on the gurney into the preparation room, and I held her little hand. She looked at me with her big blue eyes and I saw she was frightened too. There was so much for her to deal with: people, masks and air regulators, needles and smells all so unfamiliar. The anaesthetist came in and I felt sick at the thought of Poppy going under, even though I knew it was necessary. I fretted about being there when she woke up because I knew she would be scared if she couldn't see me. I imagined her freaking out and pulling the cannula from her arm. 'She's going to be fine,' the hospital staff said, but the words barely penetrated my mind.

I belong to a family of worriers; it was the only way I knew. But somewhere inside I knew it wasn't helping me or my little girl. I wanted to be fully present for my child, but I'd worked myself up and I was exhausted. It wasn't how I wanted to be, but I was completely engulfed in the feeling of overwhelm and couldn't see a way out.

After a sleepless night watching over her from the armchair, feeling awful about the huge bandage wrapped around her small head, a question popped into my head. *What would it be like if I didn't get stressed?* There was no miracle epiphany or sudden easing of the demands I felt upon my shoulders, yet something inside of me shifted. I could see the situation from a different perspective. I had gained conscious awareness. What if, instead of my mind racing to the worst possible outcomes I could imagine, I paused for a moment and considered what the best outcome could be? What if it really was going to be okay?

So many of our thoughts and reactions are habitual, operational and unexamined. According to research by Stanford University's Dr Fred Luskin, the average person has around 60,000 thoughts per day, and 90 per cent of them are repetitive.[1] These repetitive, habitual thoughts are designed to help streamline our life processes and make things easier, but they also put us on autopilot—they help us live day-to-day without being fully aware.

In that moment beside Poppy's bedside, as the negative chatter in my head reached a crescendo, I became aware enough to question the validity of my own thoughts. The reaction to this awareness in my body was visceral.

Living with conscious awareness

If we can cultivate an awareness of our consciousness—our thoughts and sense of being—we can shift the dialogue in our minds. This has the power to be life-changing.

I spent the next week playing with this idea of flipping my internal conversation. By the time Poppy's stitches were removed, I had made some progress. It was challenging—I had many deeply ingrained thought patterns to interrupt—but I tried my best to notice every time I was having a negative thought, and practised shifting to a positive one. Poppy's accident, and what I found out about myself through the experience, was trans-formative. It showed me how developing the muscle of conscious awareness could allow this to become a state of being that I lived from every moment of every day. Without worry. Without stress. Instead of sabotaging the things that were important to me, I started to elevate them by bringing conscious awareness to my thoughts and actions.

•

Conscious awareness is about becoming cognisant of your thoughts, feelings, perceptions and surroundings. Awareness cannot exist without consciousness. I could easily do a deep-dive here into the many philosophies around conscious awareness, which have occupied thinkers for centuries—but in this moment, for the purposes of our day-to-day lives, it's enough to know that conscious awareness can be as simple as noticing. This is also the most difficult aspect. It's not always easy to notice what is going on inside our minds and bodies. But it's possible. Endlessly possible.

Conscious awareness is an ongoing practice. We can't do it once and think we will be carried forever by some new force in our lives. To practise means being in a continual and lifelong state of learning and developing. You can start building your conscious awareness skills right here, in this moment, just as you would commit to developing strength by beginning a training routine at the gym.

The first step to cultivating conscious awareness is to become aware that you haven't been aware. Ponder that for a minute or two. As we seek a life of greatness, one truth cannot be disputed: we can't change what we don't see.

Meditation in its many forms, including mindfulness and guided visualisation, is an excellent way to work on your awareness. But you can gain awareness in any moment if you slow down and notice. Use your breath to anchor yourself in the moment and observe what is happening in and around you. Observe deeply—don't just look, but actually see. Slow down your tasks. Spend more time in nature—watch a river flow or a tree sway. Do some people-watching and notice in others what might be in you. Actively engage all of your senses—stop and smell a flower, listen to the birdsong, feel the sun on your skin. When you can, take the time to write down what you are noticing. It doesn't need to be elaborate and you don't need to share it; the simple act of turning your thoughts and observations into words on a page can increase your awareness.

Do nothing and allow yourself time to rest without an agenda or the ever-present to-do list. Read inspiring stories about other people or explore different philosophies. Ask yourself, 'What does this feel like for me? What are my own beliefs and biases? What can I question?' In time, conscious awareness will become part of who you are and how you live your life. Every. Single. Day.

As I became more conscious of my thoughts, I realised how many of them were negative. Negative thinking—often called negativity bias—is hardwired into our brains as a survival instinct.[2] We learn from a very young age to pay attention to negative stimuli as a way to keep ourselves safe. Brain studies show that more parts of the brain light up in response to negative stimuli—that is, our brains are shaped by negative stimuli far more readily than positive stimuli. In this era of social media, bad news and biased information, it makes sense that we've become 'programmed' to respond to the negative before the positive. By the time we are adults we are perhaps more likely to be worriers and overthinkers than we are to be positive, dynamic or even well.

As we grow up, much of this negative thinking is framed as 'caring'. Our caregivers, understandingly concerned for our ongoing welfare and happiness, may warn us of impending danger at every turn. They may quash our dreams with 'what ifs' and 'maybes', none of which are ever likely to come true. If you were brought up in this environment, you are more likely to inherit this tendency for overthinking. I know I did, despite my loved ones meaning well. When I was a child my uncle came home with a convertible car. My grandmother cried because all she could think about was that his children would fall out. We can laugh, but as adults we can also understand this as an allegory. And we can consider the old quip: 'I am an old man and have known a great many troubles, but most of them never happened.' If we bring conscious awareness to our negative thoughts, we can challenge them and realise most of our imagined worst-case scenarios are unlikely to eventuate.

One of the greatest impediments to conscious awareness is our tendency to focus on the past or worry about things that haven't happened yet. Have you ever received a work email after hours that's triggered a cascade of negative thoughts? You sit on it overnight, wondering about the hidden meaning behind certain words, imagining terrible outcomes and becoming caught in a downward cycle of anxiety and tension. We've all been there. You play over and over in your head what you might say in response to questions that you are framing from the most negative perspective you are capable of. By the time you have slept on it and you're getting ready for work the next morning, you have a whole story running in your head about a situation that may not even exist.

Your negative thoughts have shaped your experience of your world and who you are in it. Conscious awareness—slowing down to focus on the here and now—can break this cycle.

In our task-driven, output-seeking, competitive world, slowing down goes against all that we are taught about how to be success-ful. Yet the art of pausing, of taking a moment to actually stop, breathe and feel what is really going on, is a life skill that can bring you into a totally new realm, well beyond the traditional measures of success.

Everything you've ever learned about meditation and mind-fulness applies here. Conscious awareness is about catching ourselves. It is about being generous with our me-time and cultivating moments of pause—moments in which we stop, feel and name what we are experiencing. One of the most satisfying things about embracing a life of greatness is figuring out which practices work for you. Perhaps your best strategies for arrest-ing a downward thought spiral might include popping on your favourite meditation app, going for a drive, taking a few cleansing breaths, digging in the dirt or dancing to your favourite music playlist. There are many ways to embrace conscious awareness and free yourself from negative spirals.

Every tool you need for conscious awareness is already inside of you. Pause, breathe, feel, describe and then respond . . . consciously.

•

When I interviewed her for my podcast *A Life of Greatness*, UK psychologist and bestselling author Dr Julie Smith described how changing the way we speak to ourselves shifts our brain chemistry and emotional state. Conscious awareness lets us choose how we speak to ourselves and others. Words are powerful, and sometimes our greatest challenge is having the right words to say—especially when it comes to how we feel. If we work on expanding our vocabulary, we can start to more readily and insightfully name how we are feeling. Think beyond the basic descriptors (mad, bad, glad and sad) and instead approach your feelings with curiosity, rendering a more colourful, dynamic and personal understanding of what is really going on inside. How does it feel to consider words such as inquisitive, vulnerable, violated or playful instead?

If we can be consciously aware of the specifics of how we're feeling and what we're thinking, this gives us more power to decide what action (if any) to take in response. For example, if you can notice a thought and identify it as negative and inaccurate, this gives you more onus to shift it. There is power in cultivating this habit because it allows you to create the experience you want. When I find myself considering the day ahead, I ask myself: 'Am I going to focus on the positive or the negative?' This is a choice we can all make. Crappy things can happen, of course—this is not about denying the reality of some of our life situations—but where are you focusing your attention?

This really landed for me recently after I experienced a seemingly super-disruptive, out-of-control 24 hours. For weeks I had been negotiating an interview with a specific international guest. I'd worked through our different time zones to find a time in which we could both be our best. I'd researched the guest's field of interest at length, and drafted and redrafted a series of questions for him to respond to. I was excited, but I could also feel something wasn't quite right, though I wouldn't have been able to put my finger on what. On the night of the interview, it was well after 10 p.m. and we were set up in the studio and ready to record. I felt energised despite the late hour and the fact I'd already done what felt like a full day's work. I'd opened up the Zoom session ten minutes before our scheduled time and waited patiently. The top of the hour came and went. His face did not appear on my screen. Ten minutes later I texted the guest, but my phone did not buzz with a reply. Twenty minutes, 30 minutes went by. No show, no interview, no follow-up, no explanation. We eventually packed up and went home.

The next morning I made my way back to the studio to prepare for another important interview with a popular Australian guest. The interview was a delight, full of interesting conversation and heartfelt sharing. By the time we wrapped up we'd captured more than an hour of video and audio. Or so I thought. As my producer and I prepared to scrub through the video and make a few notes ready for editing, we realised the video had not recorded—none of the cameras had worked and there was no visual content. All we had was the audio.

Later that day I pulled my car up to the kerb in front of my house. Next door there were construction works—a new home was being built for a family I was yet to meet—and during the days I'd been hearing drop saws whir and tradies chat as they worked. There was cyclone fencing across the front of the property and a skip on the tiny nature strip. At 4 p.m. every afternoon there was a scurried clean-up before the site fell silent for another evening. I usually arrived home just a few minutes later, as I did that day. But this time, before I had even turned off the car, I saw it: a pile of refuse, what seemed like leftover building materials and some random pallets, had been positioned against my front gate. What the hell?

My state of overwhelm had started to take over my capacity to ride with what felt like a constant barrage of negativity. But instead of running with that, I gave myself a moment to pause and reflect. I noticed how I was feeling as one experience layered over the next. I wondered, how could I use everything I had learned about conscious awareness to shift the game? How could I reframe this series of events to help myself through?

In the good grace of a moment to pause, I gifted myself new insights that totally shifted my perspective. I recognised that, in the lead-up to the ghosted interview, I'd had an intuitive feeling about that guest. My instincts had told me something was off.

This was an important learning that I should listen to my gut. I also realised the lack of visual content from that morning's interview wasn't really a huge issue. The true value of my work is in the audio anyway, and my producers can do amazing things improvising with still photography and graphics. Then, as I got out of the car and started removing the building refuse and pallets that I thought had been dumped against my gate, I heard the lady from across the street call out to me. Although we'd never really met, she knew my name and she rushed across the road to greet me.

'Sarah, your dog was out,' she explained. 'I found her on the road. She's inside your garden now, but I had to secure your gate with whatever I could find.'

In each difficult moment I had, just as us humans do, experienced a negative response—but every single one of those moments could be reframed in a positive, or at least neutral, light. Without conscious awareness, I would have continued on in a cycle of blame and exasperation. With awareness, I could choose to see things differently and even create 'better-than' scenarios.

I went inside and took a long moment to connect with my precious dog, Lola. She sat on my lap and I patted her on the head. The gratitude I felt was immense, and any residual annoyance quickly dried up. And now I had a new friend in the street. I had met a generous, caring woman who had saved a stranger's dog. Later, when I took my sweet neighbour a bunch of flowers to say thank you, we sat and chatted about her life for more than an hour.

There were so many positives hidden within those 24 hours, but I had to slow down and make myself aware of them. We practise, we grow and we reshape our worlds.

•

The brain consists of millions of neural pathways, all with the capacity for change. We can retrain our brain to support us in following positive and life-enhancing pathways. The science on neuroplasticity is broad and irrefutable. We are capable of rewiring the propensity to negative thinking that we have learnt. It's possible to start right now.

One of the most simple and effective techniques is this: think about the things you love. This practice was a game changer for me. The things that bring us a sense of happiness are profoundly personal—but perhaps we have more in common than we think. When I need to shift my state from negative to positive, one of the easiest go-tos is to sit in my love for Lola. Consciously bringing my mini schnauzer to mind delivers a smile to my face. She's an elder at fifteen, and I love her more every day. I think of her, wherever I am, and my mood shifts. She is a beacon of positive energy.

I can also flip my switch to positive if I think about the work I love. I feel so privileged to be able to reach a wide audience, and knowing I am helping others fills me with a sense of value and pride. It's an instant positivity fix to remind myself of this when I need to.

Each of us can summon a memory or dream for the future that instils in us a sense of happiness and positive energy. If we take an inventory of our blessings—that is, if we bring all the things that make us happy, including family members, friends, creative pursuits and so on, to conscious awareness—we immediately start training our brain to focus on the positive.

When I interviewed internationally renowned therapist Marisa Peer on *A Life of Greatness* she told me most of what we worry about will never happen; as little as 4 per cent of our worries will ever take shape. We have the power to observe what we are thinking and feeling, and shift course accordingly. There is real potential for us to master our thoughts and master our worlds. Marisa said, 'You might as well tell your mind amazing things and have an amazing life. Why would you say something negative to your mind?'

Conscious awareness also helps us see events as singular presentations rather than grouping them together. During the difficult 24 hours I described earlier in this chapter, each event I encountered wasn't that much to deal with on its own. But grouped together they quickly became overwhelming. Cultivate a mindset that can segment the little dramas you experience and you will have a clearer perspective on their impact on your life.

Understanding that life happens *for* us, not *to* us, is also important. There are many thought leaders who talk about the shift that can happen with this mindset change. The Newtonian law of cause and effect says that what we put out, we receive. You need to be a better person to have a better life. You can't expect good things to happen to you if you're not a good person. And, when you behave as if something is possible, you can ultimately make it happen.

The greatest truth is this: if you want change, you need to change. It is a law of the natural world; it is impossible to achieve change by doing the same thing you've always done. What comes first, though—without question, for every living being—is the need for conscious awareness. This is ground zero for any step towards personal growth, because if you can't name what you're feeling or experiencing, how can you even begin to change it? Conscious awareness is the key to unlocking a life of greatness. You hold that key.

Chapter 3

The gift of listening

We have two ears and one mouth so that we can listen twice as much as we speak.

Epictetus

'I am listening.'

Sit for a moment and let those words soak in. They have the capacity to make you feel valued and heard—to feel that you matter and that what you have to say is important.

I have made it part of my life purpose to be a good listener. I am deeply aware of the space that is created when we practise listening in conversation. It's my job, as an interviewer and podcaster, to listen—but listening has evolved to become so much more than that in my life. I've found that, when you create the time and space for people to respond, when you place your full attention on another person, they feel free to share things they have perhaps never revealed to anyone else before. In the space of being met, real communication happens. Listening is how we create connections with others, and the empathy and understanding that flows from these connections helps us live a life of greatness.

I have, over the years, pondered this. What kind of magical, underlying power could unlock someone's heart-fuelled emotions so that they felt safe to share their deepest feelings with another in conversation? I have realised there is no special question or tactic to find a way in. Instead, it is the simple act of being a present listener.

Otto Scharmer, author of *Theory U*, talks about different types of listening. He says cosmetic listening is the lowest level of listening, where the brain is collecting words but not their meanings. Then there is downloading: listening to gather selective facts. Factual/conversational listening is where we listen in order to respond: both parties listen and speak, although one party can easily swing the balance and dominate the conversation.

If we're seeking to truly understand the other, we have to work to remove ourselves from the conversation. Empathic listening is about seeking an emotional connection. It is less about listening for facts and more about listening to understand the place a person is coming from. Paying attention and slowing down and listening without judgement are the keys to empathic listening.

Generative/emergent listening is a hybrid between empathic and factual/conversational listening. It's defined by active listening and questioning, with a focus not just on one party but the encounter as a whole. In generative listening you enter a realm of possibility, where you can form insights about the present as well as the future. This is a style of listening that holds space for new understanding. The goal of generative listening is to be open to new ideas, and this fuels the deeper listening dynamics that lead to greatness.[3]

I've used deep listening to make sense of the world since I was a child. Listening seemed to come naturally to me, emerging from the part of me that was full of curiosity. It has never occurred to me to pretend to listen. I am always there, with my full attention and without judgement. It seems these two qualities are fundamental to good listening, but it's also simply what drives me. I have always had big questions and needed answers. As a child I was constantly posing queries my parents struggled to answer: 'What happens when we die? Do horses dream? How did life come to be? What is on the other side of the sun?'

All through my childhood I was quietly absorbing other people's lives. I've always listened to everyone's stories: my grand-parents talking about their embattled past, the man towing my car telling me about his life in regional Australia, the girl at the bar sharing her most recent breakup, my friend's mum talking about her life before she retired from nursing. Something seems to happen when people realise I am really paying attention—they reveal more because they feel connected, heard and understood, and sense that I can hold space for them.

My grandfather was one of the most generous storytellers of all time. My grandparents' house was always buzzing and filled with love and togetherness. It was truly a haven for me, my brother and our cousins. Zaida (an informal Yiddish word for grandfather) had been a builder and was a very strong and devoted man, loving his wife, children and grandchildren dearly. One winter's day he decided to build a flying fox in his backyard. I watched him work in his shed for hours, marvelling as he meticulously cut wood and hammered the pieces together. Once he was done, he smiled from ear to ear and laughed as he watched us climbing the rickety stairs then swinging down, holding on for dear life. I never got tired of that flying fox and the joy it brought us.

When we would visit, Zaida would tell us stories about the Holocaust while my brother and I sat at the marble kitchen table eating our grandmother's chocolate chiffon cake.

'Zaida,' I asked, 'how did you escape?'

'My dad told me to go to Russia to find help for him, my mum and my four sisters. I was only sixteen years old, and I didn't know anyone. I followed some other people also escaping Poland. We came to a forest and when we were told to hide because the Nazis were coming, I found some bushes and hid for what seemed like hours. When I finally popped my head up to see where everyone was, there was no one to be seen. They had left me. I was alone.'

'Oh no,' I gasped. 'What did you do?'

'I started walking to Russia by myself,' he said. 'I was so frightened, but I had no other choice.'

Eventually Zaida found a house and knocked on the door. The lady was scared to let him in at first but, sensing his desperate situation, changed her mind. She kindly put his wet boots next to the fire to dry and let him sleep in the spare room. In the morning, the shoes were dry, but they had shrunk.

'I went into a panic as I had no shoes to wear, and so many more miles to walk,' Zaida explained, the anguish still obvious in his eyes. But kindness was present even in times of such darkness, and the family gave Zaida a new pair of shoes. Then, as they were fortunate enough to have a car, they generously offered to drive him close to the Russian border.

'When I arrived in Russia, I knew I needed a job. So, I became a welder and builder. We were treated poorly as refugees, and the working conditions were very hard. We were given a single loaf of bread a day for our work. Some of the men I worked with hated the work so much that, at night, they would put salt on the burns they got from the welder so they did not have to go back to work. They would scream in pain, but that was better than working the next day.'

Each time I watched Zaida's eyes tear up reliving these memories I was deeply moved by his story. His difficult journey; his determination to find his sisters, the only remaining members of this family; and his triumph when he boarded a plane bound for Australia.

In the latter part of his life, my Zaida developed Alzheimer's disease. His short-term memory was fading, yet his scarred long-term memory remained. In his final years he could barely talk. I would sit with him for hours, and I valued that shared presence as much as the stories and laughter of prior years. In the end the humble act of listening, even in the silence, brought both of us comfort. Our love was beyond words. My grandfather gave me the gift of being able to listen.

Now, everywhere I go, I am listening for stories. Thanks to Zaida I have a profound appreciation of the pauses in between and the words unsaid, and the sacred sense of humanity that exists when we really listen to one another. Listening is a psychological form of nourishment for mind, body and soul. The humble act of listening is a superpower we all have innately, inside us.

•

I've been fortunate to interview many people for *A Life of Greatness*, from humanitarians and celebrities to adventurers, innovators and wisdom-keepers. My aim is to learn what *they* think it means to live a life of greatness. One of the most common themes that emerges is the power of listening. When we hold space for someone to express their feelings, it helps us become more empathetic. Listening allows us to grow in understanding and compassion, two qualities that lead to greatness. You could say listening is a wellbeing practice unto itself. A perfect stranger taught me this very lesson.

Sharona was a kind-hearted woman who had come to my home to speak with me about her father, Ephraim Finch: the former director of Melbourne's Jewish morgue and burial society, the Chevra Kadisha. I liked her straight away. She was warm and friendly with a great big smile and easygoing demeanour. She had the kind of open-ended energy that I instantly felt comfortable with.

I had listened to her father Ephraim speak over a decade prior. I remembered how much he had devoted his life to caring for people in times of loss. I had arranged to catch up with Sharona to get some background about his life before I had the privilege of interviewing him personally for my podcast.

'Tell me about your dad,' I said as we sipped our tea. 'I want to hear everything about his life, from the very beginning.'

'You know, my parents met at fifteen and eighteen, married three years later and began their (long) path to Judaism,' said Sharona. 'They had both been brought up Christian. My mother grew up Presbyterian, and my father Anglican, but they read a book together about spirituality and Judaism and it changed their lives.' She smiled.

'How beautiful,' I said. It was rare for two people from the same religion to make a decision to convert to another religion together.

Sharona told me about some of the more challenging moments in her father's career. The stories were heart-driven, yet relayed without ceremony, as if the noble ideals of her entire family were simply a part of life. I was in awe of this woman, and I could tell that her father was observing a duty to a power greater than any of us could ever imagine.

Shortly into our conversation, the door to the kitchen swung open and Poppy appeared, with her doll and a hairbrush in her hands. She gazed at Sharona with immense curiosity.

'What's your name?' Poppy asked. 'What are you doing here?'

'This is Sharona. She is here to tell me about her dad's life. He is a very special man,' I said, a little embarrassed about how direct my daughter had been.

'Why is he so special?' Poppy asked.

'Because he has taken care of a lot of people,' I said.

Satisfied, Poppy grabbed a bag of popcorn and left. Sharona sat smiling, seemingly enchanted by my daughter's questions.

As our conversation progressed, I sensed a particular kind of silence entering the space between me and Sharona. Was there something she was not yet telling me? I was curious.

'Other than the strangers he has taken care of over the years, has your father experienced any personal loss?' I asked quietly.

I looked at her face as it started to crumple. Her beautiful brown eyes welled with tears as she divulged a heart-wrenching story.

'My eldest brother and his wife lost their first child. She was stillborn,' she answered as a heaviness descended on us both. 'Dad and Mum were at the hospital when it happened. It was horrible, and so unexpected. Dad took her body and cleaned it and put it in shrouds, like he did with all the dead he took care of. Then my brother made his own daughter's coffin. They buried her a day later.'

I found myself so overcome with emotion that I couldn't help but cry too. I had such empathy for these people I had never met. I felt a little awkward with my tears, but Sharona made me feel protected in her warmth. We were simply two people connecting on a deep human level.

'In our religion, caring for the dead is the highest form of service to another soul. It is considered a good deed because the deceased person cannot thank or repay you for the help you gave them,' Sharona explained.

We reached for the tissues together. I was not only deeply connected to Sharona's pain, but also humbled to hear her family's tale—this part of our conversation that had transcended into a communion of the highest order.

'My dad devoted his whole life to people. There were no working hours for him. It didn't matter what time of the day or night it was or what he was doing, if someone called him because they had lost a loved one, he was there,' she said.

'He took care of the bodies of so many deceased children. One mother, whose baby had died at birth, was told not to hold her child, and the body was taken away by the hospital before she could see it. Dad took care of the body, and a few months later that mother called and asked to see him. She asked him, "Did my baby look like me?" And Dad replied that she did.

'These were the stories that surrounded Dad's life,' Sharona continued quietly. 'Full of heartache and sorrow. But he took that job so seriously, and he helped so many who were mourning those they loved.'

'How did he deal with that heartache when he came home and went back to being your dad?' I asked.

'Their faces and their stories came to him when he dreamed. They are always there,' said Sharona.

I sat there, dumbfounded. What Sharona's dad had devoted his life to was unimaginable, yet it was his calling. I understood why so many people adored him. And I also realised I had connected with Sharona, who only an hour before had been a stranger, on an incredibly deep level. Through the power of listening, we had been united—and it was a precious gift of life itself.

I realised then that the stories we have the courage to reveal also have the power to lift up others. The tales of our lives, our battle scars, our losses and victories, can give others the hope they seek to conquer their own obstacles.

The conversation was powerful. A simple decision to sit and listen with empathy had brought us together in profound ways. That was all it took.

•

The gift of listening

There are many ingredients that make up the magic of listening. It starts with having an open mind and an interest not just in the person speaking, but also in the act of listening itself. It's about quietly observing others. We are nuanced people and our bodies speak as loudly as our words. Notice how a person changes their voice or demeanour around different people, or when they feel uneasy or emotional. These are the cues that a good listener can be attuned to.

Great listening has the potential to enhance our human experience. It brings us into the moment, where nothing else matters or exists except for us and the person we are speaking with. In these moments we can build a sense of togetherness and cultivate a bond between us and another that is deep and enduring.

In his research, psychologist Carl Rogers found a link between listening and self-discovery—the latter of which is essential to living a life of greatness.[4] He says when we listen with empathy and attention and without judgement, we allow people to relax and share their inner feelings and thoughts freely. We create a safe place where people can go deeper into their consciousness and discover new insights about themselves— including those that may challenge previously held beliefs and perceptions.

But reaching this heightened level of unity and self-discovery requires more than just being quiet, polite and nodding your head attentively (although these are all excellent things to practise to show you are paying attention). Active listening requires you to listen with your whole body. All of your senses can become attuned to the cues that people provide as they talk. Non-verbal communication is just as vital to conversation as the words spoken—perhaps even more so if we consider that our body language may reflect our subconscious thoughts and feelings. In this way, noticing non-verbal cues is the doorway into deeper conversations.

Watch closely and gently, without judgement, for the ways in which people's bodies reveal more information. A flutter of the eyes, a pause to look into the distance—these are subtle cues that there may be more going on under the surface. When people hold their breath, sigh, raise their shoulders or shift their sitting position, these are cues that can allow you to take a conversation to a new level—if you notice them.

Consider how you are sitting as you chat with a loved one. Leaning in to a conversation, even if only by a slight angle of the head, can show you are paying real attention. Mirroring body language can also provide unconscious feedback to the other person. If they have their legs crossed, and it is comfortable for you to do so, mirror their body position. Maintain a level of eye contact without pinning people to their chair. If you have ever come across the concept of soft gaze in yoga practice, this is another area of life in which it can be helpful. Bring a softness, a sense of loving kindness, to your gaze and your conversation will automatically be filled with a deeper sense of reverence. And of course, having your phone on silent or, even better, tucked away where it cannot be a distraction is essential.

To listen effectively, we must be kind and give the conversation space. We must give our undivided focus to the other party and listen respectfully with all our senses. We need to *feel* our conversations, and this means being present in the moment. When we allow our minds to wander, or start thinking about what we are going to say next or the answer we are going to give, we are not actually listening. Trust yourself that you will naturally and authentically know what to say next without overthinking it.

Allow space for reflection and silence, and keep your own comments in check until the other person has finished. Interjections are the quickest way to limit a conversation. Without interruptions or agendas, a conversation can flow in unexpected ways and go more deeply. It helps to keep an open mind; jumping to conclusions is a sure-fire way to shut a conversation down well before it is over.

Offering advice without permission can also affect how open the other person feels to sharing. Offering your listening ear is more about being receptive than it is about being the one with answers. Always ask, 'Would you like a suggestion?' before you bring your own thoughts and advice to the table. We underestimate the power of listening, and people's own ability to work through their thoughts when they have space to say them out loud. When others feel you are listening, they see you as a person of value and presence. These are qualities associated with the greatness we see in people we admire. Breathe in and savour every word.

Slowing down conversations is an art to be practised. The world is busy and we always have somewhere to be next. However, if we can see our conversations as opportunities to listen rather than speak, we can give them the gravitas they deserve. This extends to all our conversations—with our partners, children, colleagues and friends—but we can also practise deep listening with the service station attendant, the person scanning our groceries, the student serving our coffee. Taking the time to ask questions to show you have listened to the person, and to clarify whether you have heard and understood their perspective, is a great skill to master. When questions are open-ended and people have the space to answer in their own way (as opposed to closed questions that only have one or two predetermined answers), you are opening up the listening space. Speaking a person's own words back to them is another great tactic. It shows you want to understand them, and provides space for them to correct you if you haven't. This type of feedback is vital in real exchanges.

The beauty of great listening is that anything you do to be more present helps. You can start in this moment. Listening is a skill we can all practise; it is a simple but life-enhancing way to be a better person.

•

A few years ago, I had the privilege of interviewing one of Hollywood's greatest actors, Academy Award–winning Matthew McConaughey. This was a different type of conversation to the one I had with Sharona. It was to be a published interview, with the added pressure of it being conducted within an allotted time period, and with a man who was highly experienced in the art of media. Being able to quickly create a feeling of trust was vital. Trusted listening is not something that just happens. You need to actively build trust by showing respect, and by treating the person's responses with care. In trusted listening, you recognise that people bring their fears and vulnerabilities to you. This is to be honoured, and responded to in a way that creates a sense of safety. Bringing my whole self as a caring listener to this interview was the key.

When I start any interview, I try to establish a rapport with my guest before I press the record button, although if the interviewee is on a tight schedule, I also don't want to waste important interview time.

That day, Matthew appeared on my computer screen with his hair tied back in a messy bun. He was sitting in his office, with piles of books stacked on his couch. I introduced myself.

'Hi Sarah, I'm Matthew,' he replied with a cheeky grin and heavy Texan drawl. It was clear why Hollywood had come beckoning.

'Thank you so much for taking the time to come on my podcast today. It's a real honour,' I said.

'The pleasure is all mine. Thank you for having me,' he replied.

I sensed from the first five minutes of chatting that he was an absolute gentleman—caring, down-to-earth and real. We chatted about what was going on in the US, the election and Covid-19, and he wasn't dismissive in his answers. In fact, he was refreshingly happy to engage in pre-interview banter.

The first part of the interview went well, but he gave conventional replies. I knew within my heart there was more—that I could make a deeper connection with him in a real way. I had consciously tried to create an environment of trust. I decided to ask him about landing his first lead role in the movie *A Time to Kill*.

'I read in your book about how excited you were when Joel Schumacher and John Grisham called you to offer you the part,' I said. I'd done my research and it showed I cared about our conversation.

He recalled this unforgettable moment in his life with a big, white-toothed grin. Then, instead of asking him how it had felt or what he did that night to celebrate, something inside of me urged me to go one step further. I wanted to get to the beating heart of the conversation, beyond a simple cookie-cutter response. I trusted my instincts. This bravery is where we find greatness.

'Tell me about the moment you dropped to your knees and said "Thank you,"' I said. 'Who were you saying "thank you" to?' (This is something he wrote about in his book.)

Matthew looked at me with a glint in his bright blue eyes. He took a deep breath, and seemed to drop his guard. He then said, 'God.'

Suddenly, the interview elevated onto another plateau. I felt the energy between us change. I remember thinking, *He trusts me. He has told me something deeply real for him. I have now taken this conversation to another level.* We had connected around something important. Mutual trust had sparked a conversation about gratitude, love and heartache—a deeper exchange that would not have happened had I not been listening deeply.

When we finished the interview, I thanked Matthew for his time.

'Sarah, I loved it. I would be more than happy to chat with you again,' he said, smiling.

I was buzzing when I got off the call. I was so uplifted by our conversation. Then an email popped up on my phone from Matthew's manager. *Matthew was blown away with the interview. Thank you, Sarah,* it read.

As I sat back in my chair, I was filled with happiness. It's amazing what real listening—this time in the form of what

Otto Scharmer called generative/emergent listening—can do to elevate a conversation. It's not just being silent and waiting for your turn to talk, but paying attention to each word, each nuance, each expression. Also present in this interview was the trust required to go deeper. Trust takes you into spaces where you dare to ask real questions. You also need to trust yourself—trust that, whatever the answer, you have the capacity to respond to it, to hold it with care. When a person trusts you they will reveal a little more of their inner world.

The experience of interviewing Matthew taught me that real listening is important with all people, from all walks of life—whether I'm talking to my next-door neighbour or a high-profile celebrity. Listening and trusting creates connection, which encourages real sharing.

Wholehearted listening opens us up to self-discovery and insight, and these are the foundations of the self-actualisation we find in greatness. In these connected conversations, time will seem to stand still. Nothing else matters besides the loving energy that connects two people.

I treat all my conversations with friends, family members, colleagues and even strangers differently now. I know that every conversation has the capacity to go deep, and it happens—time and time again. Real listening has an alchemical quality that not only creates transformation, but also acts as a pathway to living a life of greatness.

Chapter 4

The art of knowing

To know thyself is the beginning of wisdom.

Socrates

Daylight was fading. Slivers of twilight splashed across the bedroom floor, creating a geometric pattern diffused by the timber plantation shutters at the window. It was a beautiful time—the meeting of day and night—and I'd always cherished this marker of another day spent alive.

I hovered at the doorway to my son Oliver's bedroom. He had grown so much, I thought as I watched him. His limbs had lengthened and his face had started to thin as he approached the next phase of his growth. I was touched to see the emerging of the man within him, and I could see tiny signs of this as he went about his life. He had always taken his role as my firstborn seriously. His room had been slowly evolving, too, from the room of a child with toys and novelties to a space that revealed his emerging tastes. At the foot of his bed was a bag of clothes ready to be donated to charity. He has goodness within him and thinks of others. He thinks of many things deeply, and his face was concentrating as he considered something far off in his mind. He stood by his bedroom window, and I called his name gently. 'Oliver, want me to close your shutters?' I asked.

I followed his line of sight, curious about what he saw. Something had his attention and he did not move, or even answer, for what felt like a long time. I moved a few more steps into his bedroom, and I saw.

He was looking across our street to our neighbours' house, where a single light burned in the front window. 'Hey,' I said softly as I joined him. I let my hand rest alongside his on the windowsill. He didn't move it away.

'She's going to pass tonight,' Oliver said. 'I know it.' He took a deep breath.

We stood in silence together for a moment as he leaned in against my shoulder.

'I believe it, too,' I said. 'Shall we say a little prayer?'

His chin dropped and his eyes softened as silent words, holy words, were spoken deep inside. I trusted his words, as I trusted his instincts. He was saddened but he was also resolute. I was caught in this moment of great beauty. Of the gentle knowing that we were part of together.

'Goodnight, Maria,' Oliver said, and he turned to look at me.

It was one of the most beautiful moments I have ever shared with my son. Beautiful and sad, full of possibility and meaning. His honesty, his belief in his own sense of things, was reassuring to me. Children have access to something some adults have lost their way with over the years. Without the experiences of adult life that, over time, dull our ability to access our knowing, children accept this capacity as part of who they are.

'She made the best biscuits,' he said. 'What are they called again, Mum?'

'*Kourabiedes,*' I said.

'I'll miss her dropping in after school with her baking.'

A few hours later I was preparing to sleep when a text arrived. We had already turned the lights off in the rest of our home, and I was in my bathroom squeezing toothpaste onto my toothbrush as a final ritual before bed. My phone buzzed insistently on the bathroom counter. *Who could that be, so late at night?* I thought, but deep inside I knew. The text was from our neighbour, Gia—Maria's daughter. *Maria died peacefully an hour ago,* the text announced on the brightly lit screen. I put my toothbrush down and stood for a long time in silence, allowing the feelings to wash over me. We had known.

Knowing is a function of the soul. When we allow it to be heard, it can give us a profound sense of momentum and understanding in our life. We might experience it as a feeling of intuition; the terms 'knowing' and 'intuition' are often used interchangeably. Knowing can encompass our feelings of 'right time, right place', and alert us to things we might be afraid to say or pursue. Knowing, whether we are aware of it or not, can drive our behaviour and shape our lives. It can set us in the direction of our life purpose, if we hear and listen to it.

In the modern world we are encouraged to dismiss our knowing in preference for facts, logic and what can be proven. It is easy to lose our connection to knowing in the humdrum routines of daily life. We ignore the voice inside us that sometimes presents as gut instinct. However, if we can lean into and learn to trust our inner knowing, we can cultivate a life of greatness with a much deeper regard for our innate wisdom.

Knowing is a special kind of non-ordinary intelligence. It's like a waking dream. To know that all will be okay is a special part of the human experience. Our inner knowing is not something that we chance across or should take lightly. Despite the questions we ask ourselves and the darkest moments that we endure, knowing continues to flicker, waiting for us to fan its flames and consume the doubt in our lives.

We start our lives with this flicker of fire but sometimes, as we move through challenges and experiences, our fire is dampened. We are told not to trust the flicker we feel inside. We learn to ignore our knowing and wonder why things go awry.

Many of us, when reflecting on our lives, can see where we have ignored our inner knowing and suffered the consequences.

The art of knowing

A few years ago I began a particular interview and almost immediately knew something was off. My subject appeared on the Zoom call messily eating a sandwich, and our initial conversation was unfriendly and disengaged. Ten minutes in I had such a bad vibe—my knowing was screaming for my attention—but I persisted for the allotted hour, perhaps out of a sense of needing to finish what I had started. When I reviewed the interview later it was unusable. It had no redeeming qualities and it did not align with my values. Had I followed my knowing I would have abandoned it as soon as I had 'that' feeling.

Even when we ignore our knowing its flicker is still there, always enduring, always waiting for us to return. The spark of knowing exists in the hearts of our children and is an urgent reminder of what we can return to. Knowing helps us create the life of greatness we want. It tells us when we are being real, when we're off course and what is true for us. This is what it is to be alive. Knowing urges us to change things. It reassures us that we can let go of the things that prevent us from living the life we seek. Knowing is our direct access line to all that we need to be true to ourselves, and this is the foundation of a life of greatness. Knowing reminds us that everything will always be okay.

I see the possibility for knowing all around us in life. Sometimes it takes a trip to another country to see how deeply embedded knowing can be in a culture. A few years ago I was in Bali on a family holiday. One morning, Oliver and I set off alone to take in some of the sights in the area we were staying. It was warm and humid, and we committed to exploring despite knowing we'd probably be far more comfortable in the hotel pool. We were both drawn to take in this beautiful place and its culture while we could.

We headed out, clad in long-sleeved cotton shirts and pants with sandalled feet, water bottles slung at our sides. We walked away from the major tourist area and out of the messy chaos of the town.

We soon arrived at Tirta Empul, a famous temple that has been the subject of thousands of photos. Water poured from the mouths of the deities embodied in sculpture at the shrine. This is a culture that has, at its golden heart, the giving and receiving of blessings, and as we moved among the people from all walks of life, we felt the sacred energy. The Balinese flock to their temples every day, and it struck me that you wouldn't do this if you didn't believe in knowing. Even when it is pouring with rain, women with babies on their hips climb the many stairs to the sacred sites; the sick and infirm light candles and incense and offer their prayers; the elders and children pay their respects; and the travellers and the weary seek out the tranquillity and safety of these sacred walls.

People come to Tirta Empul to purify themselves, to ask for help, to pray for what they need in their lives and to give thanks for the blessings they have received. It softened my heart to see this continual outpouring of love and gratitude. When I looked at Oliver, who was only ten at the time, I could see that he was open to what was happening around him. We both understood knowing as a personal endeavour, but at the temple we could see what knowing meant for a community. It was a powerful energy to be part of.

After we had washed in the temple waters and given and received our own blessings, I was feeling full of patience and gratitude. Our prayers had been heard, and now we could let go and be. It seemed to me that knowing was a lived experience for the people around us. It was a way to be for the Balinese people. Oliver and I talked about how the culture we lived in had lost so much connection to knowing. My son was lost in thought for a long time as he processed our conversation. It was an important realisation for him.

Then he said to me, 'Mum, if I gave you a million dollars would you take it, or would you double it and give it to the person next to you?'

It's a game he had enjoyed at school, and it felt potent in that moment. Answering this playful question allowed us to access our own inner knowing—to tap into something deeply human inside us. This was Oliver's way of acknowledging the lesson he had learned that day. I could see the bond this simple experience of knowing had created between us, and knew I would cherish it.

We do not need to be in a sacred temple, nor witness the delicate spaces between life and death, to experience our sense of knowing. We can reconnect to our knowing by taking time to drop into our own thoughts, by acknowledging the voice inside of us as valid and giving it permission to speak. We can think about all the times we were encouraged to ignore or override our inner voice and remind ourselves of moments in our lives when it has provided us with a source of wisdom. We can build from that, reanimate our knowing by giving it careful consideration—and then respond accordingly.

Sit quietly with yourself and seek your own counsel on life's questions and challenges. Take up a pen and journal with your own inner voice. Honour what comes out by seeing it as relevant and real. Attune yourself to the feelings you have in your body that come with knowing. It might be a flurry of the heart, a dull ache in the stomach or a propulsion towards something that you cannot explain. This will help you come to know and rely on your own knowing.

•

I'm going to create a podcast that helps people live their best life. It's going to be well received and I'm going to build it into a successful offering.

As I described in the introduction to this book, this idea arrived in my mind as if placed there by the most loving and kind mentor I could imagine. Sometimes knowing appears as a vague feeling to me, but this time I had a very specific and visceral understanding of what I had to do.

I strode into my former boss's office one morning and told him my idea. 'I want to start my own podcast. I want to share stories and inspire people to change their lives for the better. I know I can do it,' I said.

He looked up from his morning coffee and saw the excitement on my face. Behind him the window framed a scene that looked like the type of image you'd choose for a Zoom background, spanning from the city skyline to the open vista of blue skies and seaside. He didn't have to entertain me or my ideas—I saw he was genuinely intrigued. This was a big step for me and a big ask of him. He raised his glass to his mouth as if to give himself time to think and drained the remains of his latte. For a moment I let doubt enter my mind. I thought he was stalling, trying to come up with a reason to dissuade me. There were plenty: I already had a full working schedule, I was at capacity. Yadda yadda yadda.

'Put a plan together. I'll take a look.' And with that, he picked up his phone and motioned me out of the room, mouthing, 'Sorry, I need to get this.'

As I left I gave him a knowing smile. I already knew he'd green-light me. My whole body knew.

Over the next week I prepared a proposal that ticked all the boxes. My working life had taught me the steps of the dance that would get these kinds of projects over the line. I wrote my objectives, I rendered a picture of who I thought my intended audience would be, I created a format for the podcast, I described the tone of voice and the specific content I'd like to include and I prepared a shortlist of ideal subjects to interview. As far as plans went it was a solid idea, interesting and fresh, that required a big enough leap of faith to make it real. And the whole time I sat at my desk, often late into the night, putting this document together, I could feel that it was already done. This was my thing, this was my heart's call on a page. This podcast, as a unique expression of me, was going to be realised in the world. I knew it. I couldn't explain why I felt this way, but I went with it. My knowing gave me more than hope: I experienced the sense of certainty that came with deep truth. With this knowing I could actively shape my life.

I submitted my proposal with a sense of gratitude. I felt energised and ready for the next step, and I was already planning my first interview. There was no place in me for doubting; my knowing only strengthened as I took these necessary steps towards fruition. This powerful force carried me through the next few days as I waited for feedback. I rested in the awareness that there was no space for 'no'. I gathered myself together and anticipated the arrival of the 'yes' I already felt.

Meet me in my office at 5 p.m., said the email. A single line.

'You think this has got real legs?' my former boss said as I approached his desk.

'I do.'

'Okay, let's give it a shot. But you'll have to self-produce for now, and there's a few things I'll email you about. When do you plan to start?'

'I already have.' Knowing does that for you. It's a powerful force when used in the pursuit of a great life.

•

When you have lived in the same street for a long time, your life is shaped by those who live alongside you. While some houses see occupants come and go, others stand resolute, holding families for generations, their history steeped in the walls and on the pavement. Children grow up and sometimes, if they are lucky, they get to buy the house next door to their family home. The roots of family life spread under the paling fences, snaking around the garden gate to the front door. Backyards are shared spaces, and there is an endless stream of cooked meals and children running backwards and forwards between two structures that equally feel like home to them.

That's how it was for the family that lived across the street from me. Two homes side-by-side, where the boundaries were blurry and whoever was there answered the door. Many times when I went to Gia's house, her mum, Maria, would fling open the front door to greet me in her favourite spotted apron.

Our families had become close over the years, and it was a shock when Maria was diagnosed with a terminal disease. It was impossible to imagine life without her around.

There are myriad opinions and plenty of research about the usefulness of prognosis—whether it's helpful for people to understand their likely life expectancy. For some patients, having a prognosis motivates them to beat the odds. For others, it helps them plan the end of their life, prepare a funeral, make peace with their world and maybe even take one last holiday or tick more items off the proverbial bucket list. There are some people for whom the prognosis becomes a timeline, conscious or unconscious, and the passing happens closely in line with expectations.

Maria had days in which she felt good and held precious hope that she was getting better. But then her pain would return, and she would fall into what Gia called her 'resignation' that life was over. She asked the understandable questions—'Why me?'—and resisted eating.

'I think deep down she had a knowing that she was moving much more quickly into decline than we wanted to believe. She gave in to the process on many levels. Well, we thought it was giving in, but she seemed to know it wasn't a fight for her to take on at that point. But I held hope that she'd have a much longer time with us,' Gia told me.

As Christmas approached, Gia's dear friend took her hand and told her to prepare for the fact that it was probably the last time she'd spend the holiday with her mum. 'So, we will get Easter then,' said Gia. Her friend, unable to say the words no one wants to hear, hugged her instead.

That night Oliver and I stood at his bedroom window really was the night Maria passed away. It was just four months after she had been diagnosed, the exact prognosis the doctors had shared with her. It is not for us to speculate whether a different prognosis might have affected Maria's will to endure. Through the wisdom of her own life experience and the forces of her knowing, Maria sensed that her time was coming to a conclusion. Where others hoped for more time with her, Maria knew differently. And this knowing allowed her to prepare herself and her family for her passing, to accept her life as it was and to cope with the pain of her suffering. It helped her with her own mourning, and shone a light for other family members.

When I sat with Gia and her daughter Jana months later, once some of the most acute grief had eased and they wanted to talk about their precious mum and grandma, Gia shared a small bit of information that even her daughter and father did not know.

'Mum always said she knew she would die at the age of 74. For the whole of her adult life she said that, and she wouldn't listen to a word otherwise. She had a knowing that I could not shift in her despite all the rational reasons and logic I could offer her. She said she would die at 74 because that is when her own mother passed away. She was right.' Maria had found her own sense of comfort in this knowing.

My son was right, too. He knew Maria was dying that night, so he was more prepared and accepting of it. More importantly, he was able to let himself feel what he felt and process those feelings.

Sometimes we have to accept we can't know all things; however, cultivating a sense of knowing is the essence of a great life. It connects us with the deep inner wisdom that we carry, untainted by others' expectations or our past traumas and fears. It is a clear line to the part of ourselves that knows what we truly need. It is there in times of joy and celebration, and it is there to guide us with good grace through our difficult moments. It is there in all the spaces in between, steering our hearts in ways that can be silent and unknown, but also energising and real. When we feel the power of our own inner longings and express them, we participate in a life-affirming act of co-creation. We strengthen the compass directing us to a life of greatness. It's an inner instrument that no one can take away from us.

And by the way, yes, I did answer Oliver when he asked me the million-dollar question in Bali. I told him I'd double the money and give it to the person next to me. I hope it's you.

Chapter 5

Embracing your authenticity

To be yourself in a world that is constantly trying to make you something else is the greatest accomplishment.

Ralph Waldo Emerson

The street was quiet. I parked tight against the kerb, my little silver two-door car standing out in the line of family cars and SUVs that edged bumper to bumper on either side of the narrow corridor. It was autumn and the trees had dropped their leaves in a carpet of golden chaos. I had set up a playlist on my iPod and the steady beats drummed in the car speakers. It was the early 2000s and I was dressed for dancing.

The bayside Melbourne suburb was a melting pot of culture and history. The homes were solid, all period features and neatly clipped hedges. Over the decades like-minded people had gathered there, creating families, weaving stories and building a community. There was a sense of timelessness, of things never changing much, and it was both reassuring and, at times, something to strain against.

The passenger car door sprang open and Rachel's face appeared in silhouette. She leaned in to greet me with a kiss on the left cheek, her face flushed and her breath tight.

'Here I am,' she said as she wedged a plastic shopping bag between the front seats into the back of my car. 'I had to time it just right.'

Rachel was shrouded in a mass of fabric. Her skirt was long, almost to her ankles, softly draping over her body in a sea of nonchalant navy. Her shoes were what most people called 'sensible': flat-soled, simple leather, stylish but softly so. Her long-sleeved shirt was buttoned to just under her collarbone, where neat gold jewellery—her favourite necklace, a gift from her parents—was just visible. Her beautiful face had minimal makeup and her hair, one of the features she liked most about herself, was tied in a simple low ponytail.

'Are you ready?' she asked.

I looked at myself in the rear-view mirror. My smoky-eye makeup was perfect. My dancing shoes were new and fabulous. There were sparkles on my black dress, and my hair was loose and super glossy after a quick trip to the hairdresser that afternoon. I felt like me at my best.

'Always ready,' I replied.

I started the engine and checked my mirrors. A family of four in subdued clothing—the chosen attire of religious Jewish people on Shabbat—was walking slowly and purposefully on the opposite side of the street.

'Wait a minute,' Rachel said as she shuffled down. 'It's my neighbours. Let them go past first. I can't be seen.' I slouched down with her and we muffled our laughs together.

'The things I do for you,' I said. 'Where to first?'

Rachel and I had met in our final years of high school. We went to different schools but had friends in common and, as we moved through our teenage years, we saw each other out and about. We had an instant bond and our friendship developed quickly and intensely. We went from acquaintances to fast friends in the space of a single one-hour phone call. It was real, it was exciting and it was formative. We had a mutual curiosity for how life was for the other. Even today, as life circumstances see us living on opposite sides of the world, we share a bond and delight in each other. Rachel knows me for who I am, and I know her. It is a friendship bonded in authenticity, but her story is a tale of how expectations can have us living in conflict with our true selves.

I pulled my little Polo away from the kerb and pointed the car in the direction of the city.

'I need to change,' said Rachel.

'Obviously,' I replied.

I drove another five minutes until we were in a neighbour-
ing suburb and found a quiet spot to park. Rachel wriggled in
the passenger seat, wrestling with the zipper on her skirt. For the
next ten minutes she quietly completed her transformation from
Shabbat fashion forward to funky underground nightclub chic.
She tossed her skirt in the back, revealing a pair of bright skinny
pants with flashes of diamanté detailing on the pockets. As she
unbuttoned her shirt, I saw she had chosen her favourite black
slinky top for the night. I tapped two fingers together in silent
applause for her. She reached into the back and rustled in the
plastic bag. Inside were her wallet and mobile phone, and a pair
of heels. In the visor mirror she added colour to her lips and
cheeks, and a dramatic sweep of eyeliner. Suddenly we were two
young women ready to dance, just like any other teenage girls on
a Friday night.

Rachel, by her own admission too self-conscious to thrive in
the world of childhood ballet lessons, came alive on a nightclub
dance floor. She danced in bliss for hours. Her true home was
among the mess of people and beats that held the space for her.
With my already well-seeded love for hearing people's stories
I moved among the crowd meeting new acquaintances and
diving deep into the life details that made people different. It
made my heart sing. We had, for a time, found a sense of home
in these nightclubs that shaped our togetherness yet allowed us
to shine in our own territory. It was real to us. On these nights

out we were who we really were—authentic, true to ourselves and our essential natures.

•

The ability to express our true selves, free from judgement—or at least free from the fear of judgement—is liberating. It's fertile ground for relationships, and the humans in them, to flourish. The desire and ability to flourish is essential to a life of greatness. It is the force driving us to seek our full potential. Authenticity is at the heart of human experience. Yet life happens and we find our true light dulled. There is much that asks us to quell our inner longings. It might be a single event, a series of experiences or an entire life where expectations reign over self-expression. We learn that being ourselves is risky so we adapt, we adjust and we survive.

In the quiet moments that I cultivate in my day, I often think about Rachel and the challenges she faced during these tender times of becoming herself. The woman I shared so many commonalities with was also tending to another version of herself in her family life. Her role as the daughter in a modern Orthodox Jewish family was defined for her in many obvious and subtle ways. And as she grew into herself, she started to question the misalignment of her inner and outer worlds.

Usually our Friday night outings ended up back at my place. We danced, we laughed, we came home and crashed in my bedroom and slept late into the next morning. Rachel opened up to me more and more as our friendship deepened. There was one story that has always stayed with me. As Rachel told me about the defining moment in which she realised something was off in her life, I felt for her sixteen-year-old self. She was on a holiday with friends in Surfers Paradise. It was a Friday, and the tropical heat of the day was giving way to the evening breeze that was typical for that time of year in Queensland. Rachel and her friends were in full holiday mode. They'd spent the day under the palm trees at the pool and beach. They'd bought ice creams and magazines, and chatted about their plans for their holiday and which theme parks they wanted to visit most. They soon worked up an appetite—what teenager isn't always hungry?—and decided to head to a local fast-food outlet for hot chips.

After getting their chips they took them back to the multi-storey apartment complex, an imposing concrete high-rise building trimmed with white balcony rails. Rachel and her friends were engrossed in conversation as they entered the lobby. Rachel suddenly felt a sense of dread through her veins, a rush of prickly energy. *Who are those people over there staring at us?* She realised it was a family from the Jewish community back home, also on holiday on the Gold Coast.

'Oh crap, crap, crap,' she said, muttering to her friends. 'We've been spotted.'

And they were. They were 'caught' with food from a non-kosher kitchen, dressed in regular summer clothes that were definitely inappropriate for a Friday night, using a set of electric doors—the only way in and out of the building—at the start of Shabbat.

Rachel worried for days about the consequences. Being known as a girl who breaks Shabbat was shameful for her. She told me about the anguish she and her friends went through that night and in the days that followed—about being gossiped about in their community, and how deeply hurtful it was for their fragile teenage psyches.

'All we wanted was hot chips. We were teenagers feeling playful and alive. We weren't setting out to disrespect Shabbat or our families, and we certainly didn't want to hurt anyone,' Rachel told me.

This event, and the recriminations through gossip and shaming in her community that followed, were a catalyst for her. The experience pushed her to explore her wants and needs beyond the confines of her religion. I understood why, a few years later, we were sneaking her into the car and going to night-clubs every weekend. It was more than rebelliousness, more than entertainment: Rachel was finding out who she was, defining what she valued beyond her religious upbringing. She knew something needed to change. She didn't want a life of fear and regret. She wanted to explore and find what she was truly capable of. She wanted to fulfil her potential. She wanted a great life.

Rachel's steps towards a more authentic way of living were full of examination. She slowly dismantled the walls of expectation and rebuilt her own walls to support her glorious wellbeing. The practical art of non-judgemental thinking was her foundation for safe expression. Finding an authentic pathway isn't always about change; rather, it's a deep enquiry into who you really are and identifying what you stand for. This then leads to living a life of meaning and purpose. In Rachel's case, becoming more authentic actually led her closer to her religion. She has found her own version of Judaism that is rich, life-defining and fulfilling.

Rachel's mum was a special force in her life. She never responded poorly to Rachel's rebellions, instead trusting her to develop her own wisdom. She created opportunities for Rachel to think about things for herself. One Shabbat, when Rachel's mum was going to be away from the family home, she left chicken soup and candles out on the dining-room table for Rachel to find. Rachel, still in her early 20s and alive with the possibility of the house to herself for the evening, was keen to do her own thing that night. It was rare to be at home alone. But as she moved through the house, enjoying the quietude and freedom she felt, she noticed the family candelabra, the menorah, and felt drawn to light a candle.

Standing quietly at the head of the table in the half-lit room, she struck a match and leant in towards the first candle. She described to me how, alone in that room with a single flame illuminating the shadows, something came alive in her that night. She felt an immense presence surrounding her and lifting her up. For the first time she experienced a pure feeling of the divine feminine energy that is embedded in the Jewish way. She was transfixed, moved, renewed; alone but connected to something tangible, something holy and greater than she had ever known.

Her feelings about her religion gained clarity in this rarefied moment. Candle-lighting is rich in symbolism, and Rachel's mother had set the scene for her to be shown something of her own faith without even saying a word. Her mother trusted that the power of their Jewish beliefs would be present, and this helped Rachel connect with her own spirituality.

Sometimes the expectations we think we have to measure up to are non-existent, and sometimes wise people around us can truly support us in finding our unexpected truths.

To me, Rachel will always be that girl of our youth: spinning on a neon-lit dance floor, arms moving wildly in the air to the thumping beats. That is true of her. But there is also another side to her: one that embraces religion and a sense of greater purpose. In this way, sometimes our authentic self can be a reckoning of forces: past, present and future.

These days Rachel lives overseas but returns to Melbourne for extended breaks every year. Over endless cups of fragrant peppermint tea we continue to hold each other in unconditional positive regard—a space of non-judgement and the freedom to be seen. She lives with her five children and husband, embracing the very essence of her religious values—but in her own authentic way. We often talk about those days when I hid around the corner waiting for her to escape her house, party clothes in a plastic bag. She tells me her heart is glad for the life experience those acts of rebellion afforded her.

Going out dancing gave Rachel a better understanding of the world. These days, her early experiences help her connect with her own teenage children every day. 'My teenage daughter desperately wanted to go to a party with some DJs that I knew of from my own party days. I understood why it was so important to her to go and we shared a connection over this—much to her surprise. This is how my path to authenticity has enriched my life now. I am able to be in truth as I guide my own children about their own deepest longings and towards authenticity.'

One of the most important things I learnt from Rachel is to not be afraid of our own stories. This goes deep into our personal histories, but also brings us squarely into the present moment of our daily experiences. Embracing our own story in the fullness of its current reality is how we live more authentically. Rachel learnt that resisting the truth of the incongruence between her inner and outer life kept her stuck. She now makes empowered choices that align with her authentic self.

·

Do we need to be authentic to live a great life? Bronnie Ware, a palliative care nurse who has spent hours in the company of people in the final stages of life, touched on this when I interviewed her for *A Life of Greatness*. In her book, *The Top Five Regrets of the Dying*, she writes that the most common regret people express as they are approaching death is: 'I wish I'd had the courage to live a life true to myself, not the life others expected of me.'

Bronnie told me the story of Grace, a dying woman she cared for in her final weeks. Grace spent her life in an unhappy marriage with a man she described as a tyrant. Just three weeks after he was placed in a nursing home, giving her a sense of freedom for the first time, she was diagnosed with lung cancer. It was her husband who was the smoker, not her. She was angry and heartbroken that she had not lived as she had wanted. Bronnie felt her own life shift as Grace squeezed her hand with ferocity, and asked her to promise she would not give up her life in the same way. This prompted Bronnie to do a stocktake of her own life, and she realised the only thing stopping her from living a life true to herself was a lack of courage.

Bronnie shared some wisdom that I will never forget. She said to me, 'No matter how hard it is to get through the layers in ourselves that we have to heal, nothing will be as painful as lying on our deathbeds knowing we had a choice, and we chose the easy option instead of the right option.'

Bronnie urges us to be true to ourselves and find courage within. 'Be brave enough to live the life you want to regardless of what other people will say,' Bronnie says. 'I've witnessed the anguish of regret and there is no way I'm going to let myself have that experience in my own life.'

Wherever we are in our life's journey, we have the opportunity to pause and reflect on whether we're living an authentic life. It's perhaps the most important question we can ask ourselves. How heavily do others' expectations influence the daily decisions we make? How do they influence our own happiness and sense of joy?

I have often found myself living in a way that isn't true to my heart. This is a felt sense that is real even when you cannot put words to it. I feel it as a restriction in my chest and a dull ache in my stomach. Incongruence is visceral, and we can feel it when we listen to our bodies.

I grew up in a family of straight shooters and, when I expressed my desire to work in entertainment, I was quickly told it wasn't a real job. Yet I took acting lessons from age four and studied theatre at university. I loved the stage and performance, and I spent hours and hours practising, honing my skills. Later, as an adult, I found myself in work that, in retrospect, met the expectations others had set for 'real' employment. I had a career that, from the outside, looked to bring worldly and personal success. And I relished some of the jobs I worked in for a time; but eventually, the part of me that felt stuck, sad and deeply unfulfilled emerged. I wasn't in alignment. I was miserable. Something always felt 'not quite right'.

It turned out I couldn't outmanoeuvre my need to be in entertainment. I loved watching *Oprah* and *60 Minutes* on TV. I felt met through storytelling, where conversations had the power to shift the dial of public opinion, or help people grow and change. I couldn't let it go, and it wouldn't shake me either. It seemed like a miracle when the forces conspired to take me into the world of interviewing, public speaking and podcasting; but that inner longing was always there.

I believe we are born as our authentic selves. As children we have an innate understanding of what we love, what we can be amazing at, what we hold dear. Before the shadow of expectation descends on us we are perhaps the most true version of our unique selves: unformed and clumsy, yet deeply embedded in a story that is of our own making. Like Neo in *The Matrix,* all we need is already inside of us. Coming home to ourselves means living in authenticity.

•

Experiencing pain and suffering is often what triggers us to develop a more authentic sense of self. Our lives may be affected by all types of trauma, but we can shift our perceptions to create a healthier and more aligned life.

From babyhood we learn to dampen our instincts to meet others' expectations. Our survival instincts teach us to do whatever it takes to ensure our attachment to our care-givers—in both healthy and unhealthy ways. We are born authentic beings, but the society we live in, the cultural forces that provide the container for our existence and development, are broken. Our adaptations to this broken society challenge our authentic selves. Children need to be able to freely express all of their emotions: sadness, joy, anger, grief, playfulness, despair, happiness. However, the adult world requires a suffer-ing, a diminishment of the self, in order to survive. We learn not to express our emotions and, as a consequence, our natural instincts are shattered. The authentic self is crushed.

If we ask, 'How long does a creature in nature survive if they ignore their gut instinct?' the answer is, 'Not long'—and this gives us an insight into how essential authenticity is. Think about a time when you have had a strong gut feeling that you ignored, then regretted later. That feeling is from your authentic self.

Authenticity is our birthright, part of our innate, immutable self. We can feel its loss, but we do not need to feel shame or blame ourselves or others when we lose our way. We have merely been surviving as best we can. We need to show loving kindness to ourselves.

We can cultivate a habit of noticing our thoughts and feel-ings to help us identify when we're ignoring our gut instinct.

We can ask, 'Is this thought true for me now? Or is it embedded in some past experience that is no longer my reality?' Our freedom lies in our ability to choose a more authentic response in the moment.

Being authentic is learning to be comfortable in your own skin, as difficult as that might feel. If we are there for our authentic selves we embrace a solitude that is essential to our own self-discovery. As poet Rainer Maria Rilke says in his book *Letters to a Young Poet*, 'We know little, but that we must trust in what is difficult is a certainty that will never abandon us; it is good to be solitary, for solitude is difficult; that something is difficult must be one more reason for us to do it.'

We can nourish authenticity by cultivating our ability to avoid comparing ourselves with others. We can put aside our need to prove ourselves, instead recognising that it is okay for our inner life to feel like a solo adventure. It is deeply personal, but it is expressed outwardly in how we live our life of greatness.

Our expectations of others can also reflect our capacity for authenticity, which is different for everyone. Sometimes the mantra that serves us best is: 'I don't need to change anything or anyone else. This is what it is.' Live and let live. This is a peaceful place to be. Life is richer when we practise acceptance.

•

Rachel and I haven't gone dancing in a nightclub for many years (even though I am sure we could set the dance floor on fire just like we used to). Instead, we relish the ways in which we connect now as women and mothers, despite the physical distance between us. Our friendship's longevity is born of our authentic relating—the seeds we planted decades ago. We find nourishment in small, real moments in which we both feel utterly alive. Our moments together are very precious.

One Shabbat, when she was on a visit to Melbourne, Rachel and I were able to spend some valuable time together. I've always loved the park at the end of her parents' street. It's protected by a line of mature gum trees, a haven for birdlife. You can still hear the happenings of the surrounding neighbourhood—dogs, children, lawnmowers—but here in this little patch of green there is peace, too. On this day, we sat in the park and sipped from our cups as our preteen daughters played wildly with one another. They had met for the first time that day and it was magical watching them. There was a purity of acceptance of one another that spoke to me of the kind of innate authenticity that is our birthright. Rachel and I were both touched watching it unfold.

'Look at me, I'm amazing at this,' said Rachel's daughter, Georgia, as she sailed along on the flying fox.

'I'll wait for you at the end,' said Poppy. 'Then I want to do cartwheels.'

Our children felt free to be themselves, to express their own unique desires and abilities, not needing to hide or feel shame about who they were. And we realised that we were that way, too. Our friendship, deep and long, continues to open our hearts to more. And it was breathtakingly beautiful to watch our children invest in their own authentic relationship with one another, perhaps wiser for their mothers' experiences.

After some time, Georgia ran over to us.

'Mum. Please, please, please can I take my skirt off? It's getting in the way on the whizzy dizzy. I'm tripping over it and I can't run with Poppy properly. And I'm so hot.' Georgia's outfit was super cute, and appropriate for Shabbat in keeping with her family's values and traditions. Under her long skirt she was wearing a cool pair of striped leggings.

'Of course, let me help you,' Rachel said without hesitation. She seemed grounded, perhaps in a sense of wisdom from her own lived experience. I watched as Rachel helped her nine-year-old daughter with the zip on her skirt and folded it neatly into her tote bag. Her daughter ran off to play, her legs clad in rainbow colours as she leapt back on the roundabout.

'Wait for me, Poppy, I'm ready', said Georgia. 'You're my best friend.'

Despite all the differences between our children, they were still two souls finding freedom in one another, just as Rachel and I did. And times had changed. Our story was not their story.

This was a new generation. We smiled. 'Always ready,' we said in unison.

The simple truth is: we can't build fulfilling lives on the falsehoods of inauthenticity. Both Rachel and I had found our own versions of greatness—different to one another but deeply embedded in our mutual commitment to authentic relating and self-truth.

Across the playground, the girls were helping each other on the climbing frame. Two daughters, two mothers, all finding and following their authentic paths in their own unique ways. One taking off her skirt in my car, the next taking off her skirt in a playground, free to honour how she feels. I reached out for Rachel's hand and squeezed it as our girls ran over to the swings. This is authenticity: simple and real in the day-to-day rhythms of life. It is all we need.

Chapter 6

Always choosing love

Love is the bridge between you and everything.

Rumi

'I'm going to sit outside, under the arbour,' Holly said as she beckoned me to follow her with a spoon of bircher muesli. Holly is one of my dearest friends and I was delighted to be sharing a meditation retreat, on this rural property away from the world, with her. I looked around for my husband and saw him sitting with two other men, on the grass, engrossed in deep conversation. It was a big thing to take time away from our young family, but these four days were important to us as an act of self-care. We were surrounded by 100 other retreaters and the air was alive with anticipation and nerves.

'What's your first workshop today?' said Holly. Instinctually I reached for my iPhone, the one thing that keeps me organised. But there were no phones allowed in this place.

'It's called "Always choosing love", I answered. 'What does that even mean?'

'Are you ready for that?' Holly asked.

I wasn't sure exactly how to respond, so I popped another piece of fruit in my mouth and concentrated on chewing as mindful practice. The truth was, I was already feeling vulnerable.

Then it was time for us to gather for our next session. I was ready, but not ready. I was feeling thrown by some bad news about a close friend that I had received just before breakfast. I was sitting with big feelings, allowing myself to be real, and yet I wanted desperately to mask the turmoil I was feeling inside. *Sarah, this is what you are here for,* I thought. *To be real, to front up in new ways, to be love.* I coached myself, my mind whirling. *Breathe in, breathe out. Calming breaths, count backwards. Here we go.*

The room for this first session was as familiar to me as the back of my hand. There was a bank of windows looking out to a stand of trees framed by grey-toned mountains. I found an available yoga mat among the dozens that had been rolled out in perfect lines. At the top of the mat was a purple satin eye pillow and a warm blanket. I breathed in and out again, trying to push the worry from my mind.

The facilitator entered the room and sat on a simple dining-room chair. I had followed him online for a long time. I'd read his books and absorbed his ideas. But this experience—this opportunity to be in his presence and experience his work first-hand—was humbling.

I prepared myself for a guided meditation. I positioned the blanket under my head and lay down in *savasana* ready to begin. The room was a landscape of bodies lying prone in anticipation. *What is love? Where does it live in your body, right now, in this moment?* The voice beckoned us softly into contemplative thought. I tried to follow but my mind kept darting off to other things, to the bad news I was trying to digest, to the sick feeling in the pit of my stomach. I was doing my best, I was present, but I was a beautiful mess too.

At the end of the meditation, I experienced a wave of relief. It felt shorter than usual. *But what is time really?* I pondered. Except it wasn't the end. We were asked to sit up and gently open our eyes and look around the room. Without words we gathered in groups of eight. In the centre of each group was a person who had been chosen to receive our loving support.

Many of the people who came to this retreat had life-threatening illnesses or chronic pain. There were all types of people from all walks of life. There were people with walking frames, there were people experiencing major life transitions. Sometimes it was clear that people were unwell or you heard their story; other times you had no idea what lingered in their bodies and hearts and needed to be healed. I felt so much compassion for the suffering, and I was deeply moved to help where I could.

Sometimes miracles happened, and we attended knowing we were part of something greater than who we were as individuals.

A woman in our group had specifically asked to receive our loving support, and I found myself at her shoulder as we gathered around her. She was a stranger to us, but we all knew she was unwell—although we didn't know how seriously. I was unsure what had brought her to this retreat. She was lying on a low platform covered in two blankets. Her eyes were closed and she was waiting. Our mission, our offering, was to give love to the person in front of us. To gather the parts of ourselves we had found in our meditation and cherish them, to share the goodness of our hearts with openness and empathy. *I have nothing*, I thought. *I truly have nothing.*

I imagined the woman in front of me as my long-lost sister, a beloved aunt or a precious child, and I rubbed my hands together and hovered them above her shoulder. She was still. The group fell quiet; we lowered our heads and let our eyes close gently, finding the space within that we had been shown in the meditation earlier. *Unconditional love, unconditional love, unconditional love*, I chanted in my mind, though I couldn't imagine she was getting much from me as I was still feeling preoccupied by the bad news my friend had received. But I stayed there, by her side. I watched her breathing deepen and soften, and I felt the presence of the people alongside me who were also practising pouring their love into her. *Could she feel me? Could she feel love*

from me, even when I was not even sure I was capable of giving it?
Questions and doubts rolled around inside me.

We stayed centred in this practice, and the energy in the group
rose. It felt like an ocean of love. Rising and falling, bathing people
in the depth and awe that was pure love. Through the silence
I heard sobbing. In the group next to me, the man lying down was
letting go of years of grief. The sobbing came in rolling waves. It
was almost like a song. As he fell quiet, someone across the room
sighed and sighed again, over and over, hot tears pouring out with
every breath. Sometimes I opened my eyes a little and peeked at
the other groups. Everyone's heads were bowed. The feeling in the
room was of grace and beauty. One woman I could see over my
shoulder was kneeling and her mouth moved in prayer. Her
hands were gathered over her heart and the look on her face was
of glorious rapture. We were all one in love—regardless of age, of
background or upbringing, irrespective of who or what we were in
the outside world. In this space we were all equal. We were all love.
It was such a unifying feeling. We had never met before. Some
were in great pain or even dying, and yet we were all sharing in this
most exquisite moment. It brought tears to my eyes, yet there was
a part of me that remained preoccupied, frustrated that I wasn't
giving enough. I saw the traces of tears on so many people's faces.
I was not alone. The feeling of love was overwhelming.

I wondered what it was like to be the receiver of so much love
in this practice. As I pondered this, a little smile appeared on the

mouth of the woman we were supporting, as if in response to my silent question. I noticed more tears spilling from her eyes and it moved me. I sensed that this moment was the heart of what it is to be human. I hoped that she was getting what she needed from us, even though I was still unsure about my own contribution. I tried to feel love. In my mind I was repeating, *There is always more love.*

There was a signal we were nearing the end. The facilitator reminded us of his earlier invitation: to place our hands on our own hearts as a way of feeling loving presence. Gently I placed my right hand over my heart space, then my left hand on top. The room was alive, humming with love. I took a breath, and then another. On my third breath, I felt a sudden rush of warmth in my body. I realised the warm feeling was love rushing back to me through my own hands. It felt all-encompassing: a sense of intensity and softness, of beauty and life. As my hands rested over my heart, my mind was filled with the most exquisite vision. I saw my family—the people I love so deeply—smiling in front of me, and I was overcome.

Here it is again. This feeling of pure, unconditional, divine love.

It was visceral, palpable in my body.

I was on fire with the sensation of love in all its power rushing through my veins. Tears cascaded down my cheeks. Love was always there for me, all along, even when I didn't think it was. Love was there for me, for me to give to others, even when my brain couldn't connect with it. Love was there when I felt like crap. Love was there in the magnificence of daily life. Love was always there, and all I needed to do was choose it. Always choose love. That's what it meant.

The woman we had been supporting stood as we all opened our eyes. She smiled serenely. She took a moment to look at each of us in turn and said, 'Thank you.' Then, unable to contain her emotions, she hugged us one by one. She shared what it was like for her, to be bathed in so much love. Two of the group members told her of their own experience of giving. There were no barriers. She was beaming with love. Her presence reminded me there is something in human nature that is exquisitely beautiful, something that is always present even when the world is full of chaos. Something that lives in all of us; something that is the core of who we are.

That is the truth of love. That is the truth of being human. That is what we are capable of giving to the world. Love is essential to a life of greatness. When we embrace our capacity for love we live in our full potential as human beings, because love is the root of all things. It's that simple. Always choosing love is always choosing life. Always choosing love is always choosing our highest good.

•

Much has been written about love. It is the chosen subject of poets and songwriters, authors and artists. Love is a force that unites people in creative energy. It is always there and yet, at times, it can be strangely elusive. We seek it out and we are sustained by it. When it is absent, we search even harder. We don't always know where to find it, but the great masterpiece of life is that it is always inside of us. That is why always choosing love is such an integral part of living a great life.

We are never really without love, yet we attend workshops, read books and listen to music looking for reminders of it. What we think is beyond us lies within us. Love is a feeling available to all of us. The conscious choice to love more is the key to a great life; it opens us to what we are really capable of.

When we bring our attention to love, we make a conscious choice to centre our being in its embrace. This is a practice we can all master. When did you last feel enveloped in love? Can you recall a moment from early in life when love's truth dawned on you? I can.

The folds of my mum's black silk dressing gown swept against my face. I was just a child, and my head barely reached the level of her hip. She was humming as she stood in front of her bathroom mirror. I was always fascinated by her. She danced from room to room and I saw her as a queen. The benchtop was a maze of bottles and tiny tubs with brightly coloured lids. Mum's skin glowed under the row of soft lights she had installed above the mirror. Occasionally she looked down at me and touched my nose with one of her special scented creams. I would rub it in as my nostrils filled with the distillation of the many scents that have become an unforgettable memory of love. To this day if I smell something that has even the slightest hint of jasmine or sandalwood, I am transported back to this feeling of intense, pure, safe love—being loved, and loving without hesitation. It is a reflex and yet it still takes me by surprise. How incredible it is that our sense of smell and memory of love can be so deliciously entwined.

I have also come to know this feeling as a resource—a way to soften my heart and return to the original source; to drink from the fountain of love that is deep inside me. When I need to choose love, remembering my mother's scent is all it takes.

I know I am lucky to have experienced maternal love such as this; not everyone has such fond memories. Think instead of someone you trust, a dear friend who makes you feel safe. Even if we have buried our memories of love under layers of life's hubris, we can find moments that give us a direct line to the wellspring of love.

When I think about the people who I have admired for their love and devotion to the world, the faces of Mahatma Gandhi, Nelson Mandela and Mother Teresa come to mind. Faces of softness and empathy, of receptiveness and acceptance. There is a single and unifying factor that makes us respond to people like this with such veneration. These people emanate love. They emanate greatness. They have made a conscious choice to *be love*, and to express that love not only through actions and words, but in the way they carry themselves. Love radiates through every pore of their bodies.

The frequency of love draws us together. Loving connection is available to all of us. No matter what our life experiences, no matter how jaded we feel or how affected we have been by the traumas of life, at the very heart of us is the capacity for love.

I grew up believing that suffering is necessary in life; that life is not meant to be easy. There are many spiritual traditions that teach that suffering is what leads us to enlightenment or transformation, but love can be transformative, too. Transformation is one of the building blocks of self-actualisation. We can choose to be in love without having to hit rock bottom first.

We can also cultivate a practice of meeting suffering with love—not only for others, but also for our own deep aches. This is a profound act of self-care. Sending love to our suffering provides a safe passage through our fears, which can be incredibly healing. On *A Life of Greatness*, Canadian author and meditation guide Sarah Blondin talked with me about the inevitable suffering and heartbreak that is part of being human. One of the functions of the heart is to break, she said, but with love we can see our heartbreak as beautiful. The suffering that breaks our hearts into a million splinters actually has a purpose, because as we heal our hearts they expand in love. Breaking and healing is expansive. Love is the salve. And we can't stop this process. Just like the breath it continues, wired deep in our souls—a force that keeps us alive.

I find a sense of relief in this understanding of the inevitability of heartbreak. The simplest truth is that choosing love lets us step into, rather than turn from, what we are most afraid of. Coming home to ourselves is like that. So it is super important that when heartbreak comes your way, you choose love. If suffering is making you feel small, step into a deeper enquiry with yourself about how you can keep your heart open, so that your pain can be transformed.

There are many ways we can choose love. Taking a moment in my day to call up the reserves of love that live inside me and send love to another has been one of the most life-affirming, reassuring and humbling practices I have embraced. We can express our appreciation for others and take the time to affirm their feelings. We choose love when we give others our presence, so creating space is a foundation of love in action. Patience is a quality that resonates with love, as is the practice of trying to see the best in people. When we support others' passions we are expressing love, and this is also true when we show a willingness to compromise. Choosing love is about being a vessel for safety and support— how we show up in that will be determined by our own unique way of expressing our love-filled heart.

Sometimes when I need to centre my heart in love I turn to the poetry of David Whyte. Whyte's words encourage us to stay close to ourselves, to bring the secret parts of ourselves into the world. He suggests we quieten down and revive the essence of love that is part of us at birth.

Every day I make a conscious decision to choose love. Part of this is choosing to think with my heart. Heart wisdom helps me move gently through the world. When I need to return to operating from heart wisdom, I think of a particular moment in my life that moved me. I have anchored a special memory in my heart that gives me a direct line to the love that is within me. You will have a similar love story, real or imagined, living inside of you. The moment I'll share with you now is one of great beauty. It happened more than a decade ago.

I love being a mother and the births of both of my children were super special. But when I delivered my second child, I found myself in a kind of elevated state that was unexpected and magical. I had no real preference for the sex of my second baby, and my husband and I had declined to know this information when having ultrasounds during my pregnancy. Our firstborn was a boy and we have celebrated this every day. There was a part of me that anticipated this second baby would also be a boy, but we had approached this birth with neither expectation nor demand. So as I laboured, as we walked the hallways of the hospital and I practised the breathing techniques I had been taught and the movements in my hips that might help, I was not thinking about anything other than a healthy baby. All of my energy, every thought I had, was in the moment—my focus completely and utterly on delivering this baby. I moved through the stages, like every mother who had gone before me. Then, just as nature has so beautifully arranged, there was a moment when everything changed. One minute I was in labour, and the next there was a miracle and a baby was born. My obstetrician congratulated us as he delivered the baby and did the first important checks. I heard my little one whimper, and then cry. It was the most anticipated sound and I was filled with quiet relief. The doctor, satisfied all was well, brought my baby to me.

When the tiny bundle was placed in my shaking arms a moment after entering the world, I was full of emotions—gratitude, relief, joy. And then I was overwhelmed—with love and a sense of grace.

'It's a girl, a baby girl!' my husband whispered. 'I can't believe it. We have a daughter.'

'A girl, a little girl,' I repeated over and over again. 'My precious daughter.' It felt like a dream.

I was exhausted from the birthing process and yet I'd never felt more alive. I looked at her tiny eyelashes, her little fingers, her newborn cheeks, pink and shiny. I couldn't quite believe it. My husband was beaming. I felt waves of elation through my body, my mind, my heart. Perhaps it was the birth hormones doing their thing—nature is an amazing force—but it was an ecstasy that was beyond anything I had ever experienced before. I was in the deepest, most urgent, insistent, unconditional love with this little being.

I loved her.

My tiny daughter looked at me and I looked at her. She was breathtakingly beautiful. 'She has your eyes', I said to my husband, 'and my nose.'

We didn't have a list of girls' names to choose from—we hadn't given it much thought—but it didn't take long for us to name her because there really was only one option that felt right. 'Her name is Poppy,' we announced. The room was half lit, quiet and warm. The midwife looked over at us and smiled. 'What a beautiful name. Welcome to the world, Poppy,' she said. 'May you know happiness all your life.'

Every cell in my body felt love that day, and today every cell in my body can remember that extraordinary moment. All it takes is for me to pause and reflect, to animate this sense of love inside. Like an infinite resource, the birth of my child is my never-fail connection to love. I can choose love by choosing to remember this feeling. It's a resource that I hold precious, that I cultivate and turn to whenever I can. When life feels strained, or I am struggling with the demands of parenting, I can shift the noise in my head and refocus on what truly matters. Love is always there and no one can ever take it away from me.

Love is a devoted friend. It is a lifelong bestie that will always have your back.

A life of greatness is a possibility that lives inside you right now. Love makes the impossible possible. It gives you the energy to seek and embrace the best and fullest version of yourself. Love reveals you in your greatness to others. I encourage you to try to cultivate love whenever and wherever you can. Giving love freely leads to a life of extraordinary existence. It's right here, right now, in your heart and in your hands.

Centre your heart to love.

Chapter 7

Aligning with your true purpose

The two most important days in your life are the day you are born and the day you find out why.

Unknown

It was early autumn and the Melbourne nights were starting to get cooler. I was relaxing by the firepit in our back garden. When the text arrived from Jess suggesting we were long overdue for a catch-up, I immediately replied with a spontaneous invitation. *Come over. Tea at mine, 7.30 p.m. I can't wait to see you.* She was a treasured friend, one I'd been proud to know for many years, and seeing her name on my phone screen immediately reminded me how much I missed her.

An hour later, when Jess's face appeared around the corner, I beamed with joy. 'Jess, it's so great to see you again,' I said as we hugged. 'You look well. Tea for you?'

I poured her a cup and we 'cheersed' each other as we settled in side-by-side at the outdoor table.

'What have you been doing with yourself?' asked Jess.

'How about you go first?' I said. 'I have a feeling your story is much more interesting than mine.'

Jess leant in a little as if to prepare me. All of my listening instincts were alive.

'You won't believe what I'm doing now,' she teased.

Let me tell you about the time I realised Jess and I would be great friends.

I had first met Jess through her sister, and found we had many overlapping areas of interest. We'd chatted occasionally when I'd spent time at her house hanging out with her brother and sister, but it was a weekend trip away to attend an event in Sydney that cemented our friendship. There we were, in the middle of a freezing stadium with nowhere to go. We had found ourselves with prime seats right up the front. Jess hated the whole thing but her sister adored it, as did I. Jess, although the youngest, was wise beyond her years. Despite our different takes on the event, we laughed so much that weekend and made a commitment to catch up more. Jess's story fascinated me.

Jess was just fourteen years old when she took her dad to an open day at her preferred university. At fourteen, most young people are concerned with music and friends, but Jess— a confessed type A perfectionist—was already thinking about her choice of subjects and what pathway she would take after high school. She loved art and history, and she announced to her father that by the end of the day she would make a decision about her future. That day they visited the architecture and physiotherapy faculties, and it was the models they saw in the architecture faculty that swayed her. The attention to detail, the reflections of time gone by, their symmetry and aesthetics appealed to Jess much more than the images of people being massaged in physiotherapy. And, just as she had promised, her decision was immediate and absolute. Plus, her grandfather was an architect, so perhaps it was already in her blood.

And she did it. She blitzed her five-year university course, completing her masters aged 24 with several prestigious awards. Everything pointed to a grand career in design. But she felt stuck. Despite living and breathing architecture, Jess needed a prod to take the next step into a career. That came when she decided to move to Dubai with her new partner. Disembarking from a flight at 7 a.m., she was in her first job interview at 4 p.m. that afternoon. The job, for an international company headed by a design genius, was, by some miracle, all hers, and she started a career trajectory that was exactly what she had imagined. Suddenly she was the right hand for the business owner, working on master plans that would typically be the domain of much more experienced professionals. And she thrived. She rose rapidly. She was good at what she did and was respected in her field. But even back then, she started to feel the niggles of something being off. The higher she soared, the more disconnected she felt from the deeply creative material-sourcing and the feel of spaces that had been so integral to her love of the field. Romanced by a firm in Paris, she moved countries to a smaller boutique agency. She then found her way to a prestigious furniture design firm in Milan, where she could explore her love for interior design. But little by little, the sense she was not living a life she truly loved nagged at her.

Alongside all this change, Jess's relationship ended unexpectedly, and she found her heart shattered. Feeling lost and alone, she questioned everything about her life. Through the tears and pain of her separation she discovered something about herself.

'I realised I loved creative problem-solving more than I loved buildings,' she told me. 'I felt absolutely lost. Even though I knew I could always go back to architecture, I saw it as a sunk cost in my life. I felt myself stepping further and further into the unknown, wondering what my true purpose really was. I'd lost my sense of direction. I needed to find the thing that made me feel alive every morning when I woke up. It was a tough reconciliation when I'd invested so much in my former career, but I just couldn't find a sense of meaning in it anymore.'

As she rode the waves of loss, sadness and confusion, and began contemplating moving back to Australia, two seemingly outrageous ideas popped into Jess's mind. The first was that she wanted to run a marathon in one year's time. Trusting this inner wisdom, and knowing training would give her accountability for getting up every morning and reanimating her life post-breakup, she started a daily running routine. (And she did it. She ran that 42-kilometre marathon like a queen.) Her second idea felt totally left of centre. A voice inside her told her that one day her experience of this breakup would inform a book or movie.

'How bizarre is that?' Jess said to me. 'Talk about random.' The idea didn't make much sense at the time, so Jess parked it and set about rebuilding her life.

As she moved to Sydney and slowly returned to the world of dating, Jess became fascinated with how we connect with one another. Her brilliant mind, and her reluctance to jump straight back into a serious relationship, placed her in a prime position to investigate this. Without an emotional investment in romance, she was able to observe and consider the machinations of the dating world and the role apps played.

'I was heavily invested in reading personal development books and finding out more about myself,' she told me. 'I loved dissecting the dates I was having, and unpacking the experiences with my friends. It was fun, but I didn't make much of it. I didn't see it then as my purpose in life.'

When Jess chanced upon a competition where the winner was awarded a one-year gig as an ambassador for a major dating app, writing articles about dating culture, something inside of her screamed, *This is perfect.* No one was more surprised than Jess. She started writing down her ideas, and although nothing came from the ambassador competition, she did end up chatting to two guys at a party who, interested in what she had to say, offered her the opportunity to publish her dating musings on their website. Despite never thinking of herself as a writer, Jess found herself in a frenzy of passionate activity. Articles poured out of her with ease. She was insightful, the work was joyful and she felt completely authentic in doing it. And, while she was writing for herself, her articles also helped others.

'So let me tell you what I'm doing now,' she said to me.

Jess took a deep breath and leant in closer. I was intrigued all over again. What was this newfound career she had discovered for herself?

'It's definitely a leap. At one point I didn't know what to do next, but I had an innate sense it would all work out,' she said. 'So, wait for it. I'm now a dating coach.'

Her face was alive in the glow of the fire. I'd never seen her like this before.

'A *whaaat*?' I drew out my reply for dramatic effect.

'People loved my articles so much they started asking for one-on-one sessions. It just exploded. And I love it. I'm good at it. Can I tell you how much I love what I do? I'm helping people find love, get real, be true to themselves. It feels like a privilege,' she enthused.

At first, Jess resisted this new direction, thinking there was no way she was skilled or even interested enough to be a dating coach. And what about all the investment in education she had made? But everywhere she turned there were little moments, signs and pointers that this was her path. Now, purpose pulses through her. She is helping others find love, and she is learning about love for herself. And that's what she feels she is here on this earth to do. The joy and contentment are visible in her face and demeanour, and it is an honour to witness.

'What I give out comes back to me tenfold,' she said. 'I feel like it is my true purpose, my way of contributing to the world.'

From Dubai architect to Sydney dating coach, Jess found her purpose through a series of chance misadventures. It makes me ponder how, just because you are good at something, even if you are exceptional at it, that doesn't mean it is the thing that sets your heart on fire. Jess is a living example of this. She shows us how, no matter where we are in life, no matter what we have been through, there is a call in us. We have an inner knowing that seeks to send us in the direction of the thing that brings us meaning. Finding this purpose is the foundation of a life of greatness. Dream big. Care less about what others think. Optics don't really matter. Jess is proud of the help she provides to people, and she is living her most authentic life. The happiness she feels as a dating coach is a total turnaround from her previous life.

Sometimes the revelation of purpose feels like a series of random chances. But once we know our purpose, we can be more intentional with our choices. Jess took a leap of faith to action a change for the better—a change for a life of greatness. Once she had discovered her true purpose there was no holding her back. Find the thing that makes you feel your life counts.

•

The purpose of life is a life of purpose. It is not possible to live a great life without a sense of purpose; it's what sets your life in forward momentum and helps you stay on course—even when things feel hard. Commitment to your purpose leads you forward in pursuit of your full potential. When purpose is at the centre of whatever you do in life, you can begin to make sense of your existence. Just like Jess experienced, embodying your life purpose can be life-changing.

When we are open to the truth, we can see the breadcrumbs that life delivers to us along the way. When I look back on the trajectory of my own life, I see how it delivered me to my own moment of truth. Once I accepted that I wanted to be in the world of entertainment, I could step more deeply into what I am here to do. I realised that my heart's path is to serve, and that I have my own unique way of doing that. I also realised even back then that I was in a lucky position to be able to choose this for myself—that

I had supports behind me and the baseline covered, which gave me the freedom to pursue my interests. I know that is not true for everyone. Looking back I could see the many synchronicities and signs along the way. I could see that my entire career had been a process of building skills, even when I didn't realise where those skills were leading me. I have come to understand that no path is straight, but when you are on the right path, life gives you the right feedback.

Just like the famous scene in the movie *Sliding Doors,* where the protagonist chooses one path over the other, we take actions that open possibilities to new directions. When we choose the next step, we often do so without being sure of where we are going. Some of the most amazing and aligned pathways will only be revealed to us step by step. Each choice we make is an act of faith, a step towards something even bigger than we may have imagined. This is true even when we experience hurdles along the way. The breadcrumbs on our path to bliss continue throughout our lives. In my experience, when you are on the right path, when you have found your purpose, those breadcrumbs appear more frequently. Or perhaps we become more adept at seeing them and taking action in full alignment with what we are here to do.

Sometimes, due to the stresses of life or our circumstances, we are not in a position to see those breadcrumbs—and that's okay, too. If you're simply holding it together and trying to see through the dust, you may not be able to grasp your purpose right now—but I hope you can feel bolstered knowing it exists. Your life holds a promise for the future, when and if you have capacity to realise it.

I love my life as a wisdom teacher, speaker, mindset coach, writer and podcaster. This purpose came to me as an evolution in my soul. It brings together so much of what I love to do, and at its heart is a mission that I value deeply. But the road to this point in my life was anything but linear. I've had plenty of crappy jobs in which I felt complete discontentment. I've been in marketing, PR and corporate work. In my heart I knew these jobs weren't right for me, but I didn't understand why. In hindsight, each of these jobs helped prepare me for the more meaningful career I now enjoy, but at the time I often felt stuck and questioned my choices. Every day when I commuted to the office I felt rising resistance. I often had interesting work to do, but I felt removed from it.

Then, one morning just like every other, I was driving to work with my carpooling colleague when we passed a radio station studio. I randomly told her that I wished I worked there. She turned to me and said, 'You'd be amazing working somewhere like that.' Little did she know the impact her words would have on me.

I took a leap. I went home that night and did some research. I updated my résumé and found the contact details of a producer at the radio station. I emailed him a cover letter detailing my experience and expressing how much I'd love to work at the station. To my absolute surprise, I received a response quickly. Yes, by chance (or design?) he actually did have a vacant role. He asked me to come and talk to him. A sequence of events was in motion. After three rigorous interviews and a test, I got the job and it was one of the happiest moments of my life. It wasn't in the same field as what I am doing now—I started in activation and talent management—but I had my foot in the door. I expressed my interest in producing and spent many hours of my own time staying back to learn more. It felt right. And I eventually ended up in a producer role. Then one thing led to another, as I detailed earlier, and I became a podcast host. One breadcrumb—a simple comment from a colleague—set me on course to a purposeful life.

I love to talk. I love to serve. As a podcaster interviewing many interesting minds, my joy is in sharing this wisdom with others. I am energised by the simple idea that my interviews might inspire just one person to live a better life. I am humbled by the people I speak to. I feel good because it is truly and authentically me. I never imagined this would be how I found my place of service in the world. It was another leap of faith for me to move to the other side of the desk, from producer to podcast host. But I couldn't ignore the inner yearning leading me to my purpose.

People have always seemed to like opening up to me. Now I listen to people for a living, and that is such a fulfilling feeling.

My purpose is expressed through my work, but it also seeps into all aspects of my life. Purpose is all-pervasive. You can express it and live it in any way you choose. What works for me is that I'm giving back in a way that feels meaningful. I found a way to incorporate my purpose into a career, but the truth is you don't have to be career-orientated to express your purpose. It is just as relevant to live your purpose by, for example, coaching the local football team, volunteering for a community group or writing a novel.

When you're living in alignment with what is meaningful to you, it helps others get clear on their deepest truths too. Sometimes guests on my podcast respond to a query with the words, 'That's a great question.' When I hear this, I know they are about to respond from a deep and thoughtful place, and our dialogue expands in richness and value. The depth of sharing serves my listeners and has helped me to attract some amazing guests. Living and working from a place of purpose can attract great people your way, as well.

•

When you choose to live a meaningful, purposeful life, that decision will influence those around you. This includes those closest to you—such as your family, friends and colleagues—but also the strangers and acquaintances who are touched by what you bring to the world. Your capacity to live a fulfilling existence is amplified by your positive example to others. Many of my listeners have reached out to share with me how my podcast has helped them in difficult times.

During the Covid-19 pandemic, when Melbourne endured six extensive lockdowns, one of the most profound breadcrumbs I received came from a lady who took the time to handwrite me a thank-you note. I'd been having a challenging day, but it was nothing like hers. She had just had a baby, and a typically isolating time mothering a newborn had been amplified by lockdowns. She had also, devastatingly, lost a very close family member, so the joy of new life was tinged with grief and loss. This woman was, at times, so devastated by grief that she struggled to get up for her crying baby. She shared with me that she would listen to my podcast while she fed her newborn in the wee hours of the morning, and it gave her the strength to keep on going. We can never really know how we affect others, but this brave woman reached out and told me how each episode gave her the strength to face another day. This was such a blessing to me and very humbling.

When we are open to them, there are many moments in which we are reminded of our true purpose—and moments when we can send the message back to the world about who we are and what we are here for. We can let life teach us every step of the way. But sometimes we need to take chances, we need to take risks. The timing is always right even if it doesn't seem like that in the moment.

So how do you know if you are living with purpose? For me it's when I feel energised. Purpose creates its own momentum. I can have incredibly long and busy days, yet I feel totally invigorated. Purpose strengthens you, but you need to show up. You need to observe, learn and put yourself on the edge sometimes, because that is where the juice is.

Sometimes there will be trade-offs to living with purpose. Even if you understand your true purpose, it may take some time and sacrifice to see it in the world. Sometimes we just have to be in the grist of our lives and get through what we need to do to pay the bills and feed the children. Your purpose will always wait for you.

If identifying your purpose feels like a faraway idea right now, know that you can start today with some simple steps to open your mind and heart. First, go back to Chapter 2 and cultivate conscious awareness. Get in touch with your inner knowing, which we looked at in Chapter 4. Find practices that help you stop and enquire about your inner longings. Give credit to yourself as a wise being who has all the answers you seek. A sense of purpose flows from your deepest longings. Your purpose may be a new frontier, not only for you, but potentially for the world. What energises you? What legacy would you like to leave behind?

If you don't know what your purpose might be, experiment. Be open to trying new things. Start over if you need to. Take a chance to explore something new, something that has always compelled you. To uncover your purpose you might need to put yourself in different situations and explore who you are. Commit to a life of continuous improvement, understanding this will take you places you might have never imagined. Find a sense of bravery that gives you permission to try, to leap, to fly. And don't give up. I am not suggesting you abandon the things that give you a sense of security, but that you stay open to the possibilities. Keep following the calling, even if it makes little sense at the time. Know in your gut that sometimes life presents us with an opportunity that sounds silly, but makes deep sense in our heart. Trust that.

As we explored in Chapter 5, one of the greatest acts of self-love is being true to yourself. What do you think is best for you? It doesn't matter what others think or do. Look for inspirational people who have already charted this terrain. Speak with them if you can. Read or listen to their words. Speak with yourself just as you would if you were giving advice to a treasured child or dear friend. Offer yourself understanding, gentle encouragement and the opportunity to truly follow your heart.

When you need inspiration remember Jess, the woman lost in a world she had built for herself, who took a leap of faith to do something that seemed so wild but made perfect sense in her heart. These are the miracle stories, the decisions that we make every day that lead to a life of greatness.

Find what lights you up. It will be the thing that strengthens you, that illuminates your face and leads to something that is greater than you imagined. A life of purpose is more than a career decision. It is who you are. It's your offering to the world. Be courageous. We live a life of the highest kind when we find out what we are truly here for. Follow the breadcrumbs, even if they seem strange and especially if they surprise you. Find your true purpose, and a life of greatness will unfold before your eyes.

Chapter 8

The transformative nature of meditation

To the mind that is still, the whole universe surrenders.

Lao Tzu

If you want to understand how life-transforming meditation can be, you must hear Gary's story.

I first met Gary a few years ago when I attended a meditation retreat he was offering in the Vedic tradition. My first impression of him was of a tanned, cool guy enjoying the sunshine on a reclining lounge. He wore a fedora hat with the brim tipped to shade his eyes, and he looked directly at me and smiled. We had our ten-minute get-to-know-each-other session and became instant friends. Over the course of the four-day retreat, we gravitated to each other. There always seemed to be two empty chairs waiting for us at dinner. I learnt so much from him and our conversations went deep—in the topics we spoke about, and often into the night. I quickly recognised how Gary embodied all that he taught in his daily life. He lived his truth. He told me the story of how it all started for him.

•

Gary couldn't help but smile as he pressed the button on the armrest and the window smoothly and silently opened. Fresh air flooded into the car. It was a big change from his constantly-breaking-down old car, with its squeaky window wipers and mismatched panels. A brand-new company car was something to be proud of at his age—he was in his early twenties and his fashion label had a steady base of loyal customers. Life was busy, always. Gary looked again at all the dials and buttons on his dash.

This music sucks, he thought, and he started twiddling, searching for the button to flip the five-stacker CD player into action. He turned a knob, pushed three buttons in succession and turned another dial in the opposite direction, but nothing worked. The noise from the radio continued. *Blah blah blah,* incessant chatter, random sounds, jangling music. Annoyed, he pushed more buttons. The noise increased. It was torture. Pulling into the slip lane on the freeway, Gary tried to quell his agitation. It was then that he realised: the noise wasn't coming from the radio. The sound system wasn't even turned on. The noise he was listening to was in his own head—a constant stream of distraction and rubbish.

'I need to get a handle on this,' he said out loud. That was the moment he realised something needed to change.

Working not only as a fashion label owner but also as a film and TV producer, a freelance photographer and a filmmaker, Gary lived a life of feast or famine. He had work that interested him and brought him joy, but it was extremely stressful and unpredictable. Gary's introduction to meditation came out of personal crisis.

'The stress, the constant noise in my head, got so acute I had to give meditation a go. I needed to find relief from the suffering I was in,' he told me. He tried meditation in yoga classes and hated it, but the experience showed him that using a blanket term such as 'meditation' to refer to all the different practices and techniques was limiting.

'I learnt there are thousands of meditation techniques, and I started to explore. There is so much opposition in the busy mind that we really need to cycle down and settle to get to a meditation state. Not all techniques are the same or as effective as each other. Our nervous systems can be in a state of such high arousal that it takes consistent exposure for the depths to reveal themselves.'

As Gary's meditation practice started to work for him, he understood that he could bear witness to his thoughts. 'I realised

I was not my mind. My whole world opened up from that,' he said. 'Bearing witness allowed space for the traumas of the human experience to be cleared, for healing to occur, for the purging of what didn't serve me. I realised everything you need is inside you.'

It was during a meditation session that he heard a message from what he calls his higher self. It was an unmistakable instruction that one day he would teach meditation. 'I got the clear message to drop everything and devote my life to teaching meditation,' he explained.

At the time this was a risky move. This was before meditation became mainstream. There was no real career path he could reference. 'I had to support a family and a lifestyle. Back then meditation was more a fringe activity for forward thinkers. It wasn't in the media or the vernacular or even an aspiration like it is now, where we have science-based evidence that it is beneficial.'

But by then meditation already had Gary. 'I'd experienced a place inside me that I never imagined existed. It was such a state of bliss and serenity. Often I'd just start laughing. I got into it. I was fascinated to explore this experience inside myself. And it turned off the noise.'

Noise was at the centre of my experience, too. Many years ago, I was working extremely long hours in a job that consumed me and dictated the terms of my life more than I liked. I spoke about it earlier in the book—how I had already worked many hours before other people's days had started. That is the life of a breakfast radio producer. I loved my work, but the pace was not truly sustainable.

The first sound I heard every morning was my phone demanding I wake up. Of course, I'd found an alarm tone that I thought was pleasant to wake up to, but it hadn't taken long for it to become annoying. As I completed my morning get-ready-for-work routine I also moved through a regular practice of turning on the noise. The radio was on in the bedroom, the TV on in the kitchen. From the minute I rose I was in listening mode, my ears tuned to the latest news headlines and what was going on in the world. I even had a waterproof radio in my shower so I didn't miss anything. My job needed me to be on top of things, and an endless media stream was my way of being informed. I never drove to work in silence, but flipped between the radio bulletins and interviews. Once I was inside the office, our content filled the halls over loudspeakers. There were banks of TVs where we could watch multiple channels at once. I was surrounded by noise, and I thought it was normal. I needed it. It kept me focused, and always switched on. What I didn't realise, at least not consciously, was that I was being constantly bombarded with negative information. The news is full of (mostly) awful things and I was ingesting it around the clock, but never digesting it. It's hard to process anything in that much noise, and I was immersed in it for hours, every day. Noise blocks other things out. Noise keeps us from ourselves and from diving deeper into our own thoughts.

Julia, my colleague, had been a steady witness to my over-whelm. I valued her perspective on the ways of the world and often found myself agreeing with her in conversations, or in meetings. Chatting one morning in the staff kitchen, she gently asked me what I was doing to take care of myself. I laughed out loud. That is when she suggested I try meditation. Part of me thought, *Great, another thing to add to my to-do list.* But another part of me, that wise voice inside of me that I could occasionally hear through all the noise, agreed with Julia. I decided to at least try. But where to start?

Start wherever you are. There is no one way to meditate, and finding the practice that works best for you is all part of the learning. That afternoon when I arrived home to a still and quiet house, I went into my study to take ten minutes for myself. I picked a random guided meditation from a streaming service on my phone, and set myself up with a cushion, a blanket and a comfortable chair. I pressed play and took a deep breath. Relaxing music filled the air, and a quiet voice started to speak. Low, monotone words floated around me, encouraging me to draw my attention to my feet, to feel them relax, to breathe into the next part of my body and progressively relax from the tips of my toes to the top of my head.

I tried so hard. But my mind was full of gibberish. Thoughts bombarded me. They were there and then they were gone, without any sense or reason. It was like I had opened the door to the most chaotic part of my brain. My thoughts were so rapid that at times I felt like I was hallucinating. This wasn't how it was meant to be.

I wanted to get meditation right, but it felt like a far-off concept for me at that point in my life. I struggled. At times I felt incredibly bored. But I persevered. I meditated occasionally, sometimes once per week, at best every other day. Julia's gentle advice had stirred something in me and I couldn't shake it. I tried many different kinds of meditation, different practices, different sitting positions, silent, guided, long, short, this music, that toning. At one point I actually decided I couldn't meditate. My mind just didn't seem to be cut out for it.

Then came a moment of truth. Something gave way. I got a new job, and before I started it my family and I took a break together to reset. The palm-fringed beaches of Hawaii called to us. On that holiday I made one simple promise to myself: to 'be with myself' every day and meditate every morning without fail.

My husband bundled up the children for some poolside fun as I put the 'do not disturb' sign on the doorhandle. Like a port of refuge in a busy life, I found an eye in the storm, present to me when my eyes were shut. There in the tropical beauty of a small Pacific island I reclaimed something of myself. In the warm breeze that kissed my bare arms and the constant scent of frangipani and coconut, I found a sense of home within that gave me renewed stillness and peace. I found a meditation practice I liked, one that resonated with what I needed and how my mind worked. I kept with it. I wasn't perfect at it, but I built myself up in tiny steps, just a little more each time. The gift I gave myself, to show up each day, was transformational.

·

It is pretty common for people to try meditation and decide immediately that they don't like it. Our monkey mind, the part of our brain in endless chatter, can come up with a million reasons why sitting still, or slowing our thoughts, is a waste of time. I get it. We live in a culture of productivity and doing. We have schedules and KPIs and pick-ups and appointments. A dedicated meditation practice does not always slide easily into our way of being, and it takes practice. Just like learning any new skill, we must discover and grow in meditation. We must soften and receive, and let ourselves make mistakes and have unexpected experiences. In a world where goals and achievements can feel like the heart of our value, it can be a real challenge to embrace something that sometimes feels so nebulous and non-linear— something so deeply personal and unexplainable. It can be challenging to find the right words to adequately convey what is even going on in a meditation practice. But it is profoundly felt: a moment of sacredness that is often beyond the measure of sentences or even thoughts.

I am not sure when I first started to notice that meditation had begun to work for me. When I reflect on the way my practice has developed, I have had several moments of pure calm. One of them is a truly special memory that I'll tell you about now.

I was sitting in my study. Across my knees was a special blanket that I considered my meditation blanket. I had got into the habit of placing it gently over my lap, regardless of the weather, every time I sat. Even if it was a warm day, the weight of this blanket across my thighs represented a moment of 'going in'. The feeling of its soft merino fibres was deeply satisfying to me.

On this day, my meditation was a process of centring my heart back to unconditional love. I had relaxed into a beautiful awareness of the endlessness of nothing and everything. I journeyed deeper and an image arose in me. Tears began to trickle down my cheeks. I saw my parents cradling a tiny baby in their arms. She was brand new and their faces were resplendent with love. They gazed down at their little one, amazed by her delicate features, the miracle of her existence, the pure light emanating from her that illuminated the room. The energy of love was everywhere and it filled me. It took me a moment to realise, but when I did, I began to sob joyful tears. This tiny baby was me. I was being shown my own uniqueness. I felt my essential self:

pure love. Describing this ecstatic moment, even after years of thinking about it, is still a challenge. But this is where meditation has taken me. Moments like this steady my resolve to continue.

Gary told me his own story of being at one with his essential self. He was out on the water in Sydney Harbour, surrounded by the vastness of the ocean as it met the sky. He was with a group of friends, laughing while they took turns kneeboarding behind the boat. As he took a moment of quiet at the bow, he felt a shift. Another dimension seemed to open inside of him and he became a witness to his own self. He describes it as a profound state that lasted for several hours, even when he got back to shore and sat on the sand savouring the feeling. No one else noticed it in him, but he felt a deep connection to source and a state of bliss he can only describe as a feeling of enlightenment. This happened in an eyes-open state, but he knows that his regular eyes-closed meditation practice had built that pathway for him. He likens regular practice to a rising sun: developing gradually over time, a smooth ascent into a higher state of consciousness, which then bursts through on occasion.

Once you commit to a daily meditation practice, how do you make it stick? The key for me, as I suspect it is for most, is consistency. Meditation is for the mind what exercise is for the body. Meditation works best as a habit, a considered and regular part of the day, non-negotiable but flexible—as essential as brushing your teeth or doing a workout. An alternative to drama, a reward for being you. I have heard some meditators speak about book-ending their days with a practice in the morning and before retiring to bed. Others find time during a lunchbreak, or rise before dawn. I'm not sure the circumstances matter as long as you are making the choice to meditate, and being there for yourself in whatever way works best for you. Showing up is the key. And the more you meditate, the more you want to meditate.

Getting the family on board can also be helpful in cementing a daily practice. My children have grown up knowing meditation is a special part of everyday life. They have embraced their own short daily practices when they wake up in the morning. And they know that when the door to my study is closed, there can be no knocking or interruptions.

My life reshaped itself around my meditation practice. I started to notice things that I interpreted as feedback. I felt a sense that I was on the right track, and I received insights about the next steps I should take. The inspiration for *A Life of Greatness* came to me during a meditation. I found I could trust these insights as coming from a place of deeper wisdom. There is a simple truth to acknowledge: the things we experience in our eyes-closed meditation state are integral to our eyes-open life. There is a beautiful symbiotic relationship between the two.

Meditation allows us to witness our own thoughts. That shift in perspective is why meditation is such a vital part of living a great life. Meditation allowed me to understand my thinking, after which I could *change* my thinking. Once I realised the aim of meditation was not to empty my mind, but simply be with my thoughts, my practice shifted significantly.

When I meditate, I am not seeking quiet—although there is a calming of the mind. Rather, I am entering a space of deep listening. This means I notice my thoughts and feelings, and let them move through me without judgement or seeking to change or action them. I just sit with them.

This act of deep listening is fundamental to a great life. It is an act of self-love and self-respect. It allows us to process the traumas we carry and work through things we perhaps didn't even realise were there. It is an act through which we learn to trust ourselves and understand that what needs to come will come. When Socrates said our remit in life is to 'know thyself', perhaps he was also encouraging us to meditate.

In almost every interview I conduct for *A Life of Greatness*, the conversation turns to meditation. I loved speaking with Jack Kornfield, one of the world's most beloved Buddhist and mindfulness meditation teachers. He spoke to me about the importance of always maintaining a 'beginner's mind' in meditation—that is, to remember we are always learning, and that we flourish when we remain open and don't focus on outcomes. He likened our thoughts to clouds that come and go, and I found this metaphor helpful. For Jack, meditation is about trusting that what needs to be understood will come. He said that in stillness—the clearing in the forest of our minds—we see things we've never seen. Our job is simply to notice, and to see the connections between the things we are noticing from a place of graciousness and wisdom.

Sharon Salzberg, another of the world's leading Buddhist meditation teachers, likens meditation to attention and awareness training. She sees meditation as an anchor, a way of grounding and being present to experiences; a way to explore sensations in the body and transform them. She suggests that looking inwards is a lifelong process in which we develop our capacity for loving kindness and self-compassion. Meditation practice becomes a resource, a way of interacting with the world—not simply a passive activity but an active way to be alive to your life. She talks about meditation being a democratic act. It doesn't cost anything besides your time and your ability to sit or lie; it needs no special tools. Any person is capable of meditation—old, young, sick, well, from any religious denomination, of any gender, at any stage of life, experiencing any challenge or joy.

I have found myself using meditation to soothe myself. If I am anxious or worried about something, meditation can help me quickly name what I am feeling and do something about it. I recently received an invitation to a meeting that I knew was going to touch on a difficult topic. I immediately felt anxiety rise in my body. I knew I didn't want to be feeling that way. Rather than ignoring this feeling or trying to smother it with distractions, I chose to sit in meditation with it. Prior to the meeting,

I closed the door to my work office and gave myself ten minutes to sit quietly, to breathe and prepare. I couldn't change the situation, but I could change my engagement with it. As I sat and focused on my breathing, I felt a sense of peace and acceptance wash through me. I left my office and arrived at the meeting feeling grounded and strong, centred and with myself. When meditation is a regular habit for you, it can also become a resource you can use at any time.

And it can change your life. One of Gary's students came to learn meditation as a way to manage the three or more panic attacks she was experiencing per day. She had tried so many treatments: cognitive behavioural therapy, medication, other forms of meditation and counselling, all without success. Then she learnt Vedic meditation. Within six months her panic attacks had all but disappeared. Now she has maybe one a year, and she has the tools to manage it when it arises. She triumphed over her situation. Her nervous system healed and harmonised. She says she owes her life to meditation.

•

Daily meditation is a gift to yourself. It can be anything you need it to be. Sometimes short practices are just what I need; I have also come to know and value the space for longer and deeper practices at other times. People ask me how I find the time but the truth is, I am not sure who I would be without it. I feel the benefits of my practice every day. It feels essential to my health and wellbeing. It gives me greater capacity to navigate and dance through life. It is good for me.

And I want to share with you that it's not always easy. Sometimes meditation sessions don't 'deliver'. They might feel wasteful. Sometimes I avoid meditating because I know there are strong emotions below the surface and I may not want to be with them. It's my experience that it is harder to go into meditation when you have difficult stuff to deal with. But this is the time when it is most useful—when it can truly carry you. Sometimes it's the only place to go. There can be a million reasons not to meditate, and yet we do it. We show up and the beauty is there, unfolding gently as we give ourselves space to be with what is, rather than turn from it.

Establishing a meditation practice is about finding what works for you. There are so many different forms of meditation and I encourage you to experiment and see what fits. Some meditations are flexible, others are more prescribed. Try different apps or online meditations to listen to; find a teacher to study with; invest in a course or attend classes. What works is different for everyone. It may also feel different depending on the time of the day, of the year, of your life. But meditation heightens something in you no matter who you are and what circumstances you're working with. The practice will make a difference.

In meditation I am with myself. These six simple words have become a foundation, a building block for my life of greatness. Establishing a regular meditation practice has given me more than I ever imagined. It has helped me open my heart and mind, and to deepen and grow in my relationships with others. It has given me new insights into myself and provided space for my mind to fall into a natural place of relaxed creativity. It holds me, and it soothes me. Meditation unites me with the sacred dimension of life and equips me with the capacity to enjoy life more—in all its different colours and flavours.

All those years ago, Gary helped open my eyes to how meditation could help me access profound inner peace, and a stillness that is always there. Nothing else in the world can touch this part of me in the same way.

Nothing can give us immunity against the ups and downs of life, but meditation is a grounding force that gives us a stability from which we can meet each challenge we're facing.

Mediation is the most forgiving friend and an honest companion. It is a place to fall in love with yourself and your life, and to know yourself as blissful, free, whole, happy, relaxed, centred and in touch with your true being. Make a quiet space for yourself. You deserve it.

Chapter 9

Creating kindness

Kindness is the language that the deaf can hear and the blind can see.

Unknown

The round kitchen table looked out over a small terrace. I could see clusters of terracotta pots filled with the colours of the season: yellow daffodils and jonquils bursting through the soil announcing the coming of spring. As I paused to contemplate my thoughts, I was reminded of how long I had been coming to sit at this table. For almost a year, every Sunday afternoon at 4 p.m. I had come to this house in St Kilda and sat at this kitchen table, resting my arms on the floral printed tablecloth covered in PVC. In the centre of the table was always a jug of water with thin slices of lemon floating on the surface. It was thirsty work, all that talking, all that thinking, but I loved it. On these afternoons I was the student of a rabbi who, among other things, taught me about kindness.

As a person of Jewish heritage, I found myself drawn to learning about Kabbalah—a discipline and school of thought in Jewish mysticism. I was hungry for knowledge but as a nineteen-year-old from a non-denominational school I didn't know where to start. At the time there were several famous people such as Madonna and Demi Moore talking about their studies of Kabbalah, but I didn't know anyone in my own circle who was intrigued enough to study it. This didn't deter me; I felt driven to explore Kabbalah and felt I had an innate knowing about it. Then a friend suggested I approach a rabbi she had heard about: Rabbi Dr Laibl Wolf. Not only was he one of the better-known rabbis in Melbourne, but he was renowned throughout the world. And in his infinite kindness, he shared his wisdom and time with me.

It had taken weeks for us to set up our first meeting. I called and left messages about five times, and perhaps my persistence was part of his decision to welcome me into his teachings. He usually only taught in groups, but for some reason, which only he can explain, he responded to me with generosity and set the Sunday timeslot for us. On reflection I realise how absolutely privileged I am that he took me on. It was completely from the goodness of his heart. In many ways I was an outsider, but he embraced me and my desire to learn. He devoted his precious time to me. We would read the texts of the Zohar and he would patiently discuss the essence of the teachings and how they applied in everyday life. I was fascinated.

'Sarah, what do you think is the difference between sharing and kindness?' he asked me one day. This was typical of his approach—to present a deceptively simple question that holds much richer relevance when you go deep.

I thought for a minute before answering. 'Well, if you are sharing what you have, then you are being kind, right?'

The rabbi smiled. 'A simple oversight, often made,' he replied. 'The spirit with which we share is important to consider. We can share, but if we don't have an open heart then there is no kindness. Kindness can only be given when we share with an eager and happy heart.'

'So, cultivating a desire to share and being kind without thinking about the obstacles in our way is true kindness?'

'You can't just tick the box and move on,' the rabbi responded. 'True kindness is felt. It is more than just an action. It is an act prompted by something in you, not outside of you.'

One of the important tenets (or *Sefirot*) of Kabbalah is the attribute of kindness. The *Sefirot* is a series of ten attributes of expressions of the divine that guide the values through which the principles of Judaism can be expressed in daily life. The word *Sefirot* is related to 'sapphire', a gemstone that is brilliant and illuminating, implying that the function of a *Sefirot* is to give light.

The *Sefirot* concept of *Chesed* captures the idea that kindness is an act that has no cause. Often translated as 'loving kindness', *Chesed* means giving oneself fully, with love and compassion.

There is an understanding that the world is built on kindness, and that giving kindness is, in fact, what we are here to do. Everyone is connected to everyone else through *Chesed*. The concept of *Chesed* appears in the Torah more than 190 times, indicating the importance of giving love without boundaries, definitions or limitations.

Chesed is related to purity and honour. It's a giving without expectation. This is the kindness Rabbi Dr Wolf gave me, without the expectation of any return. His teachings influence what I do as a teacher today. His generosity rippled through my life, and into the lives of others. It helped me see, experience and appreciate the world in a different light.

When I spoke with self-described kindness scientist Dr David Hamilton for *A Life of Greatness*, I was fascinated to hear about the science behind feel-good acts of kindness. David's observations of the placebo effect helped him understand the importance of the mind-body connection. He told me that, according to his research, kindness is physiologically the opposite of stress in the body. Feelings of stress create the stress hormone adrenaline, which has a proven negative impact on the heart. Kindness, in contrast, generates a feeling of elevation.[5] When we feel or act kindly, we experience it as a warmth, a connection, a generosity that produces oxytocin, the 'love drug' hormone. This is an important cardiovascular hormone that protects the heart. So when you are kind, your brain produces a chemical that protects your heart. Your arteries soften and expand in size so your heart doesn't have to work so hard. Kindness can literally improve your health and wellbeing, your longevity and your happiness.

•

Our capacity to be kind is unlimited. Some people have a natural instinct to be thoughtful and generous, but we can all bring our awareness more fully to kindness, making it a daily practice. It might be as simple as pausing for a moment before we say or do something and ask ourselves, *What is the kindest thing I could do right now?* When I embraced this practice for myself, my life changed. When I practised kindness it increased my own happiness—and it made others happier, too. When a neighbour in our street had her first baby, I prepared a simple and nutritious vegetable soup and took it over to her. She answered the door wearing the sleep-deprived look of any new parent, but her face quickly fell into a state of relief and gratitude. Her eyes welled with tears as she expressed how lovely it was that there was such good in the world. I see the young man who lives a few doors down regularly bring in the rubbish bins for our elderly neighbour as a gesture of kindness. Recently, while I was waiting in line at the petrol station, a man was unsuccessfully searching his pockets for his credit card. I was touched to see the lady ahead of me in the queue quietly pay for his fuel and wish him a happy day. His face broke into a huge smile as he accepted a stranger's kindness.

It is a joyful thing to give to others without expecting anything in return. It makes us feel good, and it inspires others to practise more kindness too. That is the ripple effect that makes kindness such a game changer. Our generosity is a seed that goes out into the world and creates something new. It creates change, beauty and positivity. Kindness is fundamental to a life of greatness because it helps us create or strengthen bonds in relationships that matter. It builds the feeling of community that is essential to our sense of belonging. It helps us develop trust in our ideas and actions.

As simple as kindness can be, it is a force that expands exponentially. When it comes to generosity, there is no place for notions of scarcity. To live with kindness is to cultivate a mindset of abundance. We can give all we want, and we will always have more. We will always be replenished.

·

In nature, kindness is everywhere. Larger trees provide shelter for younger saplings; the food chain is fundamental to the nourishment of all beings and plants; humans and animals gather together in tribes to meet their needs for love and belonging. The way we express kindness to the natural world is also a measure of our humanity. When I think of being kind to nature and specifi-cally animals, I can't help but bring to mind my childhood friend Sofie. When I was young I went through a stage of being obsessed with horses. My beautiful parents supported me in my passion and diligently drove me to a local horseriding centre for a lesson every Saturday morning. That's where I met Sofie. She was a few years older than me, and every time I needed help she seemed to be there. She would appear at just the right moment to tighten the girth on my saddle or help me carry heavy hay bags. I noticed how absolutely devoted she was to being kind to the horses, as well as any other animal that crossed her path. She was always last to leave the barn because she checked all the horses' water troughs one last time before she got in the car. She had pats for every horse she met and they gravitated to her, calling out to her from the paddock. She was the type of person who always put out seeds on her bedroom windowsill for native birds. She often had a box in the corner of her lounge room for an injured bird or lizard that needed her help. Her gear bag was plastered with stickers advocating for the abolishment of live animal exports and the banning of cosmetic testing on rabbits.

Over time, my passion for horses was replaced by other pursuits and I lost touch with Sofie. But then, 25 years later, as I flipped through a lifestyle magazine while waiting at my dentist's surgery, her unmistakable smiling face beamed out at me from the glossy pages.

Sofie's kindness to animals had become the centre of her life and work. The article told the story of the animal rescue centre she had established in the hills outside of Melbourne. Sofie took on the abandoned and neglected, the unfairly treated and the unloved, and she gave them a second chance at life, nursing them back to health and helping them regain their confidence and sense of place in the world. And this had opened the doorway for her to train as a counsellor and animal-assisted therapist. Every year she saw hundreds of clients in need who benefited from working with her rehabilitated horses and other animals. She had helped war veterans come to terms with PTSD, young children with ADHD learn self-soothing techniques, and burnt-out corporate executives rediscover their life missions. Animal wisdom and kindness had helped Sofie transform so many lives. Sofie's kindness to animals had been life-defining for her, and her compassion had become a light in the dark for others. This is the power of kindness.

We can expand our understanding of what kindness is by acknowledging all the words that we can use to describe it. It's a simple concept that has many layers. If we consider words such as 'gentleness' and 'compassion', we can connect more fully with the emotions that live within us that help us show up in kind ways. Our capacity for sympathy, for thoughtfulness and for living with a benevolent heart is present in our actions, small and large. When we show consideration to those around us and provide solace in times of need, we are enacting kindness in the world. When we pause to see ourselves in the larger picture of humanity, we can see the connections that unite us despite our differences. Kindness exists across all cultures, all religions, all philosophies and all ways of viewing life. It keeps us real, and it serves a much higher purpose. The universal nature of kindness underscores its importance. Every true leader in this world shows a capacity for unlimited kindness. There are so many examples of this we can model ourselves on—whether it be a coach from your local footy club or a well-known community leader.

Smiling is a small and cost-free action that is available to every person. It's an immediate display of kindness. When we smile at a stranger or take a moment to grin at a loved one, we infuse their world with love. Smiling has proven to be one of the most powerful ways we can connect with and express compassion for others, and it has a contagious quality that can be amplified, returned or passed on.[6] Being offered a genuine smile at the right time can change a person's day. It may even change their whole outlook on life. There are countless stories of people who, thinking they have nothing to live for, have made different choices because someone has shown them an unexpected act of kindness.

Life is constantly presenting us with opportunities for thoughtfulness. I've found, though, that the busier my schedule is, the less likely I am to be purposefully generous. When I slow down a little, and cultivate moments to consciously pause and observe the world around me, I see the glimmers of possibilities for kindness. For me, paying attention to others' needs is the first step to carrying out caring acts of generosity. I start from the position that everyone around me is in need of something, because that is the truth of life. It's about noticing when people are struggling, or when life has thrown them an unexpected challenge. In my experience, these are golden moments where my compassion and insight can be of real value. Find opportunities for gestures and seize the moment to help others. Kindness can be as simple as providing ease in another person's life. We need to become great at elevating others' lives in small ways. When we truly see others and seek to understand what is going on for them in life, we can be there for them. Our support doesn't have to be material. Our presence is a beautiful gift of kindness that can be highly appreciated. It only takes our time. Be a good listener and offer your willing ear or your reliable shoulder to cry on. Be the type of person who can be confided in. In this way, kindness adds immediately to your capacity to live with greatness because it fosters connection. Let your kind actions show that you are someone to turn to.

•

When I interviewed Robin Sharma, a globally respected humanitarian, leadership expert and bestselling author with more than

20 million books sold, he shared with me an act of kindness that was, on reflection, instrumental in shaping his life.

Robin has achieved incredible things and helped people all over the world to live well. However, by his own telling, his childhood was far from the ideal set-up for developing a great leader. A child of immigrant parents, Robin mostly felt like he didn't fit in. He didn't experience the silver-spoon upbringing some other children did, and he came to believe he wasn't anyone special. His teachers did little to change his self-perception. When he was in middle school, the principal took his mother aside and told her that young Robin showed no promise. There were several other teachers who weighed in on this crushing assessment, warning her that Robin lacked any potential.

But there was one teacher—Cora Greenway, who taught Year 5 history—who believed in him. Despite others' negative commentary, she had kind words to say about Robin and his future. She saw in Robin abilities and aptitudes that no one else could fathom, and she told him this. She was generous and she championed him. Her kind words still ring in his heart decades later.

As Robin found out, it only takes one person to believe in you to change the way your life unfolds. Cora told him that if he made the right choices, he was going to do interesting things with his life. Enveloping him in kindness had a profound effect. Robin has never forgotten the way she made him feel big, boosted his confidence and helped him realise his own potential. In this way, Cora's kindness has created a legacy the world can enjoy. It seems Cora had always been an inherently kind person. Robin later learned that when she was younger she was part of the Dutch resistance, saving young people from Nazi death camps. For her, kindness was a way of life.

Giving kindness is essential to living a life of greatness. Kindness can change the way you see yourself and what you can do in the world. I am grateful for the people who have been kind to me—they have, often unknowingly, shaped my life in special ways. Kindness has provided me with opportunities and encouraged me to try new things. Kindness has been embedded in many of the great moments and memories of my life. We often don't realise just how powerful kindness is in creating change and opening possibility. These are the essential building blocks of greatness.

I have made myself a promise to always practise kindness with those who work with me. In practical terms, I offer praise. I'm careful with the words I choose when I give feedback, and I try to surprise those around me with tiny acts of appreciation. I make a conscious effort to see people for who they truly are and what they do. I recognise that I have a matter-of-fact approach to life, so I have to be mindful to slow down and look deeper into a situation, to open myself up to what's possible. By being aware of my tendency to straight-shoot, I can give myself space to pause and prepare before I speak. I think about how my words might land for the other person, and try to speak in ways that elevate people whenever I can. This creates safety and respect, fosters good feelings and builds thriving relationships. Kindness lets everyone win together. It's powerful because it meets a fundamental human need.

•

Practising kindness to others is central to a life of greatness, but it is also super important to practise kindness to yourself. It's harder to appreciate in others what you can't appreciate in yourself. Self-compassion is an important first step—at the very least, it helps you fill your own cup so you always have something to give others.

Self-compassion in action means softening the voices inside that are full of blame or shame. It's about feeling into your own humanness and showing yourself the care and love you want to show others. Self-compassion means choosing kind words when you talk to yourself, accepting your mistakes and honouring your successes. These acts build the type of compassionate heart that renews its capacity for love and kindness again and again.

It can be a challenge to practise self-compassion when we are experiencing difficult feelings, but kindness can help us move through these emotions with grace. It is often easier to show tenderness to our loved ones than to ourselves, but we can practise releasing ourselves from self-judgement as a first step. Going easy on ourselves and being considerate of our own needs and feelings is important. Being critical is the opposite of kindness.

Letting judgement go may even come with a sense of relief. How long have you been beating yourself up?

Write a letter to yourself acknowledging your strengths, or journal about your feelings and ideas. Make time to check in with yourself. How are you feeling? Do this as often as you can until it becomes a reflex. Try not to avoid your emotions; instead honour them by naming them and exploring them. There is such richness in simple practices like this.

Self-compassion both requires and builds inner strength and resources. Rather than being narcissistic, it is a way to develop coping skills and invoke a sense of calm. Build yourself a reper-toire of activities or rituals that help you feel good—a walk, a special cup of tea, reading some poetry that nourishes you. There are many tiny moments in life we can cultivate in the search for enhanced self-compassion. Kindness helps us create the space to know ourselves better, which is an essential element of a life of greatness. Over time, practising self-kindness will become even more effortless than you dare imagine.

As I have focused on being kind to others, I have found myself surrounded by even more kind people. Good people naturally gravitate towards other kind souls. There is a magnetic quality that builds a feeling of mutuality and community. When people go out of their way to help us, we feel that as kindness. When we press pause on the world and sit with a friend and really listen to their story, when we offer our help without being asked or quietly support a stranger behind the scenes, we are engaging in a quest for a kinder world that carries us all. Call someone out of the blue. Tell them you've been thinking about them and that you 'see' them. The ability to empathise is at the heart of kindness, as is patience and listening. We cannot move towards a life of greatness without these qualities.

So often we think kind things about others but keep them to ourselves. What would it be like to reach out and let someone know what they mean to you? Offering praise and acknowledgement creates an environment where people can flourish, and it builds your own sense of worth in real and practical ways. Lead by example—in the workplace, at home, in your community. It will change your view of the world.

Make kindness a habit—your default for how you carry yourself in the world. Live and breathe kindness. Kindness doesn't have to be big or life-changing; small acts matter just as much. Share what you have, show gratitude and experience the world as an abundant place. I don't think there is such a thing as too much kindness.

It's a simple and natural law: being kind brings greatness your way.

Chapter 10

Acting with intention

The intentions you set today determine the path you tread tomorrow.

Unknown

Whenever I need a second opinion on something, such as an important speech I'm writing or a major decision I'm facing, I have a reliable and wise go-to I can consult. My husband has a viewpoint I value immensely. One reason for this is that, in every decision he makes and action he takes, he holds one important question front of mind: 'What is my intention here?'

My husband's ability to embrace intentionality in his day-to-day life gives him an elevated perspective on what matters. His viewpoint rises above self-interest and grants meaning to the mundane, so that even the most basic question becomes an opportunity to lean in to a space of higher authority. At the most fundamental level, he lives his life understanding what he wants from every encounter he has. And, even more importantly, he knows how his decisions and actions contribute to a greater sense of purpose in his life. I witness firsthand how this enriches his interactions, his relationships and the way he sees the world. Living with intention is essential to a life of greatness.

When I ask his opinion on my writing, his first question is: 'What do you really want to happen?' When I pause and shape my thoughts to consider the outcome I am seeking, a magical sense of alignment falls into place. Thinking this way means nothing is left to chance, and I hold true agency in the actions I take and the decisions I make. My husband is a wonderful mirror for me, and you can hold up a similar mirror to your own desires and actions.

The word 'intention' comes from the Latin *intendere*, meaning stretching or purpose. It invites us to reflect on life with deliberation and clarity of mind. And while planning and goal-setting are often associated with intention, we can consider a much grander (yet simple) interpretation of the word when it comes to a life of greatness. Purpose gives direction to your life; intention gives shape to the moment-to-moment choices that you make. In other words, intention helps to guide you in the daily expression of your life purpose. It is at the heart of every decision you make.

Living intentionally often means stepping back from external expectations and letting go of outward-focused definitions of success. To live with intention is to have the courage to look within yourself to learn what you stand for in the world. It is a permanent undercurrent guiding your life of greatness.

Sometimes people may naturally live with intention, but more often we find ourselves living an unintentional life, saying yes to opportunities and bumping into challenges without any true consciousness or understanding of the bigger picture. That is, until something happens that forces us to take stock. This is what happened to my friend Liv.

Liv and I met almost a decade ago when we were both exploring different meditation practices. We saw a light in each other that drew us into a close friendship. We've shared many hours together on the mat in meditation, and in those lively conversations about life you can have with someone who sees things the way you do. I have learnt so much from Liv. She is openhearted and vulnerable in her sharing. We have walked many hundreds of kilometres along the beachfront near her home, chatting as salty sea spray and sunshine caresses our faces. She is a heart friend, a treasure, a wise counsel—which is why I was so moved to hear the story of her life in the years before we became friends. Her ability to turn her life around came from a considered choice to live more intentionally.

Liv, by her own admission, is one of the strongest people you could ever meet. When her parents separated when she was fifteen, Liv found an inner fortitude that was half survival mode, half 'I got this'. She was for the most part 'her own parent', often living alone in the house and taking responsibility for getting herself through Year 12. Her mum once commented that despite her being there, her daughter rejected all her offers of help and support, and presented such a capable front that there was neither need nor opportunity to intervene. Liv has always been one of those people you don't question or doubt.

Liv went to university and completed a double degree in business and marketing, followed by a Certified Public Accountant (CPA) qualification. This landed her an incredible job in London and led to a flourishing career in finance across a range of industries. She enjoyed success beyond her wildest dreams. Her instinct to survive was a present and driving force in all she did. She told me how she was always chasing more money to support herself and to help her feel a sense of security and stability, and how much she resisted the idea that she would ever have to rely on someone else. Her intention was always to have money.

In her late twenties Liv met Ben, a fellow busy professional, and they married and had two children. She had a busy working life that required loads of travel, yet Liv found herself also taking care of all the home-based duties. Her overwhelm started building in unison with her resentment. She became more and more unhappy, but she couldn't find the voice to express how she was feeling. Instead, in an attempt to soothe herself, she looked for escape hatches. Alcohol was a crutch she often turned to as her nervous system became more and more shredded. In a permanent state of fight-or-flight, she became enormously reactive. She started hurting people with careless words. She crossed lines and she betrayed herself to keep the peace. She cried easily and often. Yet for the most part she looked to have it all together. Material success was a great cover-up.

Then one day, Liv imploded at work. She walked out of a meeting where she'd had the difficult task of retrenching people. Trying to handle a family business where the boss had died and no one was getting on was more than she could cope with. She stood up from her place at the boardroom table and simply walked out, never to return. She couldn't do it anymore—physically, mentally or emotionally—and she resigned.

That day, Liv had a powerful realisation: she was never living her life in the moment. She was always projecting forward. She had enough self-awareness to realise that how she was living wasn't working, and she decided to do something about it. She felt a shift inside her as she recognised she was living without intention. Her survival could only be assured if she shifted her focus from 'money' to 'change'. This represented a seismic turn-around in her way of living.

Slowly things started to reshape. For some time, she hadn't been able to stand being in her own mind with her thoughts and feelings, but her family helped to ground her and she resisted the urge to run. She bravely stilled herself, and felt all the discomfort of being unemployed and having no sense of identity. She started to question who she really was.

Soon, she adopted a new intention: to find ways to be a better version of herself. Her search took her to a yoga teacher training course, where she learnt how to self-soothe with breath and movement instead of alcohol and work. Every day that she invested time in herself she found a deeper connection to intention and what it meant in her life.

When she discovered meditation, she set an intention to dive deep. She made a commitment to herself to meditate twice every day and to turn her attention away from the noise of her life. For more than five years she focused on peeling back the layers. Intention kept her accountable and present to this life-changing decision. Her simple choice changed everything.

These days, Liv uses intention as a guiding principle in all that she does. She can barely remember the person she was: stressed out and living blindly. Intention has created a sense of flow in her life. It has taken her to a place where she feels good and has a new sense of her own power. Instead of searching for stability and security in all the wrong places, she can flow in her day-to-day life without the need to actively strive towards particular outcomes.

If you asked Liv what her primary intention is now, she would tell you it is to be a good person. Today she is guided by an intention to use her time in a meaningful way to serve the world. Every moment of her day is devoted to this life-affirming ideal.

Acting with intention

Liv is an amazing yoga teacher. She is there to serve her students by doing the best she can. Her identity now is very different to the striving professional she used to be, and she marvels at how much she can trust life these days. She resists advertising her classes and has no desire to achieve any type of 'guru' status. She knows if she puts her intention out there, she will attract whoever needs to find her; and if someone wants to learn, she is there to share the practice. She doesn't need to push anymore, and the sense of relief in her is palpable.

Intention has helped Liv understand what she doesn't need, as well as what she does. She has found that if something is not evolutionary in nature, if it doesn't add to her purpose, it tends to fall away. The bonus? Intention has over time become more and more effortless and spontaneous for her. She can trust the opportunities she is presented with. Now when Liv receives an invitation to a social event she checks it against her intention. Does attending the event feel aligned or not? When someone requests her yoga teacher services, instead of responding with an automatic yes she considers whether the opportunity will help her serve the right people. It isn't about money anymore, and saying no has become an empowered process.

Liv's suffering has dropped away. Her appetite for drinking alcohol has disappeared. When she questioned how alcohol was serving her, and whether she even really liked it, she realised it wasn't something that added to her life or her mission. Now she no longer drinks at all. Liv has found time and time again that the things in her life that don't serve her simply disappear.

Many of us walk through life as if we are blindfolded. To reach inside and find out what is really important to you is an action that can only enrich your life of greatness. Without intention, your life may be full of needless suffering; with intention, you have a profound opportunity to live consciously, in alignment with your deepest values. Your life can transform from a random series of events into a path that extends towards the horizon of your own making.

As Liv discovered, finding stillness in meditation is a direct link to within. When you cut through the noise you can discover the true nature of what lies deep in your heart. Everything you want, based on your pure intention, will come to you with greater speed as you are willing and receptive to the magic. You will see synchronicity and possibilities in everything. The world will open up. Anything becomes possible when you live with intention. A powerful question to begin with is: 'What can I create in my life right now?'

What started for Liv as an intention to change evolved into a way of being. She discovered that deciding to change how you are living is an intention in itself. She also set an intention with her husband to look after one another, and she believes this saved her marriage.

•

Acting with intention

Intention illuminates your path forward. It helps you feel more comfortable in your own skin. You make your own life and luck. You live with expansion and joy in your heart rather than fear. When crap happens you feel more equipped to deal with it. You can move steadily towards your purpose, because intention clarifies the steps along the way. You can live in flow, and this becomes a beautiful and softer way of being.

As you evolve you become more perceptive. You begin to see reality and experience truth. Your capacity for love and your sense of empathy and compassion increase. Self-interest becomes secondary to a greater good—all this from the simple act of setting intentions for your life.

Every morning Liv wakes up and asks herself: 'How will I serve today?' This is an intention I, too, hold dearly. This book you are reading now is a testament to that.

Writing this book blossomed from my desire to help others. I didn't just want to produce a book; I wanted to serve more people and support their quest to live a better life. So many things become possible when you live with a sound intention to serve. There are no limits to what you can do. Sharing myself in this format means this information will land in different ways with different people. It expands my sphere of connection, and lets me share personal stories that I may not have the chance to articulate in other ways such as on my podcast. Writing helps clarify what we think and feel and fosters new insights. There is a beauty in writing that places the essence of the self into every sentence. I feel alive just thinking about what I can write about. Books also have a solidness to them. They are infused with the wisdom of the writer, with years of thinking and doing. Writing this book is strongly aligned with my intention to serve in so many ways.

I believe daydreaming and intention are closely linked, even though they seem conceptually at odds. Those idle hours when we allow our minds to wander and enter spaces where our creativity is not curtailed by the realities of time can foster new insights into what is driving us deep inside. Giving ourselves space to daydream can help us find or reconnect with the reasons we are here. Time for unstructured thought can give clarity and solidity to our intentions. Sometimes we have to open our minds and hearts completely to let our intentions surface.

If we don't purposefully set intentions, our unconscious intentions will influence our life. If my unconscious intention is to avoid standing out, I will make decisions that keep me playing small. Taking time and making space to enquire into and set our intentions helps us work with our true desires rather than against them. When we are not living in alignment with our intentions, we can experience life as a series of misfortunes, as happenstance. We relinquish control of one of the most powerful forces we have within us. Intention is a direct way to own your authentic power, as it informs the way you think about and respond to the things that happen to you. Intention helps you get super clear about your approach to life. It helps you develop perspective and big-picture thinking, and it steers you towards your purpose.

But how do we actually go about setting intentions? For some it can be a daily ritual. Every morning as I prepare for the day ahead I say a particular prayer to myself—one from Paramahansa Yogananda, an Indian-American Hindu monk and yogi who introduced meditation to millions of people around the world. I have found great sustenance in this statement, which, when translated into English, reads: *Spirit, I will reason, will and act, but please guide my reason, will and actions to the highest and best things you want me to do.*

There is something about speaking intentions out loud, declaring to the world what you want, that makes it real and keeps us accountable. Gary Zukav, teacher and author of the bestselling book *The Seat of the Soul,* shared some wisdom about the power of declaration when I interviewed him for *A Life of Greatness*. He told me that we have the capacity to shape our own lives through the choices we make. Literally, we create our lives based on what we focus on. To live with intention we need to be aware and responsible, and act as an authority in our own lives. Gary asked an important question: 'Why would we not take the opportunity every day to create positive experiences that feel good?' He said simply being aware of our choices and the intention driving them helps us experience our lives differently. We change our world by changing our actions. To Gary, this is a simple law of cause and effect at play. Intention shapes everything. Articulating our intentions helps us shape our destiny and identity. We cultivate a sense of control over our lives via the only type of causality we can truly rely on.

When I observe people around me who seem to be super lucky or experiencing ease in their life, I often notice they have a clear grasp on their intention. That's not to say they don't deal with curveballs, challenges or things outside of their control, but with intention there is a sense of grace in facing challenges and finding solutions. There is no secret here; the way in which intentional people navigate life simply comes from a more centred place. Intention helps us make sense of everything that happens to us.

You have probably already figured out that purpose is closely entwined with intentions. Having a clear purpose helps you set intentions with ease. I like to think of purpose as the compass for my life—the 'where to'—while intention is the 'how to', the steps I take towards my purpose. How you deliver on your purpose depends on your intentions. It is vital to have clarity in both domains, and this becomes easier the more we invest in knowing ourselves. Over time your intentions and purpose may overlap and meld together. This is a sign of a life lived in alignment— a life of true greatness.

Your purpose is what you ultimately want for yourself in your life. It is your reason for action, your reason for being.

Your intentions make up your blueprint for how to act, how to move forward, how to meet your purpose. There is immense personal power in asking yourself, 'What do I really want?'

Defining your intentions can bring to light what is missing in your life. If there is a gap between the actions you are taking and the actions that serve your intentions, this provides insight into the parts of your life that are ripe for attention and change. If intention and action are not aligned, living a life of greatness will be challenging.

Intention also helps us decide where we give our energy so we're living for our greater good. How often are you swayed by others who may not consider your needs? Imagine a life in which you only do what you intend to do. Saying no becomes easier, and there is a momentum that feels magical and right.

When you live in this way, before taking action or making a decision you can ask consciously: 'What do I want out of this?' You can give yourself the time and space to consider the outcomes of your actions and whether they align with your intentions. With this comes a sense of responsible advancement, where you live with consideration. We can garner incredible strength when we give power to our truth. It becomes so much easier to be strong, reliable, honest and real. I see this every day in my husband's life, and it strengthens us both as we live and dream together. When we live with intention, this inevitably helps others as well. Intention is where our commitment to the greater good can flourish.

It can shift the focus from the individual to the collective—meaning we are less self-absorbed and more open to altruistic ideas and actions in our lives.

Intention has an energy that provides clarity, direction and meaning to all that you do. When you cultivate a practice of intentional living, you can bring a sense of true purpose to your days. You can nurture your instinct for greatness on a pathway that is uniquely yours. Conscious intention is a powerful life skill that is worth mastering.

Everything we decide for our lives today sets the tone for our tomorrow. We have the opportunity to live a remarkable life when we set intentions. It takes time, but it's a true affirmation of what is meaningful to you. Determine and live your intentions every day and you'll set your compass in the direction of your best life.

Chapter 11

The fullness of gratitude

If the only prayer you said was thank you, that would
be enough.

Meister Eckhart

'What makes your life rewarding? What makes you feel most alive?' I asked my friend Lisa one morning over coffee. I was curious because Lisa always has such a calm, reassuring energy about her. She has an inner light that draws people in. She always seems content with what she has; it shows in her demeanour, in her actions and on her face. Her answer surprised me. She didn't tell me about her latest achievement, or that she had discovered a new skincare regime. Her answer was both much deeper and simpler.

Lisa shared with me the daily routine she credited with her happiness. Every morning, before she sat up in bed, as soon as she drifted into consciousness, she took a few minutes to make a mental list of the things she was grateful for. She aimed for five different things. Some days it was a stretch, while other days the list came to her easily. She explained that she never judged what arose in her to be grateful for. She let each item on the list be as simple or as complex as it needed to be. Sometimes she was grateful for the fresh mango that she was going to enjoy for breakfast; sometimes she was grateful for the home she had to live in or the special people in her life. She did not rise until she had made her list, and she did not go to sleep at night until she had reflected on her morning gratitude list and how her day had gone. The practice, she discovered, was like tending to her own internal gratitude garden. Every morning she nurtured the seeds of gratitude by taking the time to name them. During the day, these seeds quietly took root in the fertile soil of her life, and in the evening she could see the growth around her. She found the more she devoted herself to this practice, the more she had to be grateful for. The routine of it bookended her day and the benefits rippled through her life, creating an inner harmony that she carried with her.

Giving her precious energy to gratitude every day changed Lisa. She didn't need to actively add more good things into her life—the simple act of acknowledging what she already had made her more aware of her blessings, and had a magnetic effect of bringing more her way. She even had fun with it. And it showed.

If we don't have gratitude for what we have, it's difficult to achieve greatness because we will always be searching for something more. Life will simply never feel good enough.

There's plenty of research confirming the value of identifying what we're grateful for. It helps us see what is there rather than what isn't. Gratitude is a powerful motivator, an essential dialogue and a willing friend.

Modern psychology talks about there being three types of gratitude.[7] The first is an emotion—a more temporary feeling that comes from receiving. Think about the way you respond to receiving a gift, a compliment or a favour from someone. The emotion you feel when you write down a daily gratitude list is a good way to understand this. The second type of gratitude is experienced as a mood. It's a state that lives inside you and reflects the things happening to you as you move through your day. Then there is gratitude as an affective trait. This is our overall tendency to have a grateful disposition—to be in a state of grace that permeates our being each waking moment, and the sense of self that we occupy. This is a form of gratitude that is all-encompassing, that endures all things and has the capacity to be truly life-changing. To embrace gratitude beyond the daily practice of a gratitude list and transform it into a life-affirming and embodied practice is key to a life of greatness.

It's easy to feel and express gratitude when life is going well— when your needs are met and you have loved ones around you.

But how is it humanly possible to find gratitude in life when all is taken from you? When I interviewed Bruce Bryan for *A Life of Greatness* I was beyond curious to understand how he could be such a gracious and grateful person despite his life experiences. His story is a powerful lesson in finding gratitude even in the darkest times. He told me how affective gratitude—that is, gratitude as a state of being rather than just a passing emotion—helped him find his purpose and endure almost 30 years of false imprisonment.

A child of West Indian immigrant parents, Bruce grew up around Queens and Manhattan in New York. He was raised in a secure and happy family filled with love and integrity, where the importance of education was a deeply held value. His own parents had only attended school until eighth grade. His neighbourhood was full of families, but he only had to pass down the wrong street to find microcosms of other worlds, worlds filled with drugs and crime.

In Bruce's experience, being a young black man meant living with racism and violence. One day, while he went to the shops to return a Halloween costume he had bought for his niece, Bruce found himself being arrested. His crime? It was alleged he was involved in the shooting of an eleven-year-old boy who had been an innocent bystander to a horrific act of violence. Bruce, who was only in the area to return the costume, had been seen talking to the main suspect prior to the shoot-out. His presence there was enough: enough for him to be charged and sent to prison for almost three decades, despite his innocence. In a world where corruption and the need to make someone pay has profound implications for marginalised people, Bruce became a victim of what he calls the criminal *injustice* system. He describes his conviction as the day the air was sucked out of his life, and that of his family.

Prison life is a brutal existence for most inmates, including Bruce. Many in the prison sought the security of gang membership to survive. Violence was everywhere, and all the failings of society were present in the prison world: drugs, suicides, murders and beatings. Bruce described how hard it was to maintain a sense of humanity, but he says that faith and gratitude got him through.

Continually protesting his innocence, he found a small group of fellow inmates who were also dedicated to maintaining their integrity and values. These like-minded people were willing to participate in self-help groups and study, making the most of their time inside. Bruce would never be grateful for being locked up, but he found a way to express gratitude for the life he could make for himself while wrongly incarcerated, and it saved him: emotionally, physically, mentally and spiritually. Gratitude practices helped him build resilience and hope, and Bruce credits these with altering his experience of the world. 'I wasn't going to serve time, I was going to have time serve me,' he said. 'I always knew I never belonged there in my heart, so I never internalised the values and bitterness that existed inside those walls.'

Bruce held on to his family values. He embraced spirituality and the Bible, and he wrote affirmations and letters to God, constantly expressing gratitude for all that he had. He joined the Resurrection Study Group and learnt about the history of the prison system, of people of colour, of public figures and of America more generally. He also focused on becoming an educated man, earning his Bachelor of Science.

'I would internalise and deposit into my subconscious mind the things that were important to my soul,' Bruce said. 'I'd name what I was grateful for, and repeat the scriptures that I wanted to envision for my life. The thoughts I had when going to sleep at night would be the things that I woke up with on my mind, and they'd carry me through the day.' Bruce also meditated on his hopes and his aspirations. 'I read a book one day that said whatever you put into your mind before you go to bed you can bring to fruition. I practised this, and it was powerful.'

During his incarceration, Bruce wrote between 10,000 and 20,000 letters to legal entities asking for help. He was determined to prove his innocence. He wrote pages and pages documenting his case and seeking assistance to have his conviction overturned. He never gave up. Finally, following a series of lucky events, a high-profile lawyer took on his case. Bruce fell to his knees in gratitude and cried, overjoyed and filled with new belief.

For three years, Bruce's lawyer worked for his freedom and finally, in April 2023, a miracle occurred. Bruce walked out of the prison, his conviction overturned. He had served 29 years.

Bruce has gratitude for so many tiny things in his life as a free man: the stars in the sky, caring for his family and walking on grass. He is back living in his family home with his mother (his father passed away while he was in prison) and he relishes all the things that he visualised for years while he was inside. 'I always saw myself doing things on the outside. I always valued freedom. Now I am knocking things off my life checklist like swimming with dolphins, seeing the world and sharing my story to connect with others.' He has learnt that giving your time to the people who mean the most to you is one of the greatest acts of humanity. At night he lies next to his mum as she falls asleep to give her his time.

I felt incredibly humbled by Bruce's ability to be gracious in the face of so many challenges. He is a wonderful example we can all look to.

•

There are many physical, mental, spiritual and emotional benefits associated with the practice of gratitude. Just as Bruce experienced, gratitude can not only help us survive but also thrive in whatever shape we find our lives in. It contributes to a sense of resilience, helping us deal with traumas and stressful situations.

It helps us deal with the ups and downs of our emotions, enhancing our capacity for empathy and sensitivity. It helps reduce feelings of depression and contributes to a greater sense of wellbeing. Gratitude helps us see the greatness in our life and embrace all that we have.

Our relationships will be transformed through the presence of gratitude. There is no reason to hold back. Everyone in your life, even strangers, will benefit from your sense of grace and appreciation. It's a softer and more loving place to land that will help you deepen your connection with friends and family members. One practice you can start today is to actively think about and recognise the particular qualities people around you have. Appreciate their accomplishments and let them know. A beautiful thing happens when you do this: your words raise them up, and you also feel connected to your own accomplishments, which increases your self-esteem.

Feeling thankful can enhance your mood and boost your immunity. Research shows it has a measurable positive effect on depression, and helps you cope with anxiety and even deal with chronic pain.[8] It will also improve your sleep. Gratitude is the ultimate act of self-care and the perfect way to pay it forward. Gratitude helps you reconcile your past, brings a sense of peace to your today, and gives you a vision for the future.

•

The fullness of gratitude

My grandmother, Susie, taught me most of what I know about living life in the fullness of gratitude. I have always felt touched by the way she offers her presence to those around her, and by her willingness to acknowledge and appreciate what she has. For my whole life she has modelled what it is to live a grateful existence. When my grandfather passed away, the loss of her lifelong partner was immense for her and the whole family, but my grandmother never outwardly lamented this loss. She simply offered her thanks to him in every conversation in which his name was mentioned. She showed our family that we could focus on what we had rather than what we had lost.

Model the graciousness you see in others. Look to the people around you who exemplify a life of gratitude. It might be your grandpa, a mentor, a treasured aunty, a parent or a wise friend. Observe their ways and infuse what resonates into your own life. Just being in the presence of people who express gratitude will enhance your own sense of grace—this is what my grandmother has done for me.

Sometimes gratitude arises when you least expect it. One day a few years ago, I received an unexpected phone call that required immediate action. An opportunity I had been chasing for several months—to meet with and interview a really interesting guest— had finally come to fruition. The only catch was, I had to do it that day, and I had to travel several hours to country Victoria to meet her at her home. I hastily reset my day, arranging for pick-ups for my children and rescheduling other appointments. I was feeling on top of things and was excited to get this interview underway. I entered the address into my GPS and set off for the drive. If all went well I'd make it just after lunch and we'd have an hour, maybe even two, to chat. My mind was whirling with the questions I longed to ask and how I wanted the interview to run. I made a mental checklist of the things I would need to remember. I thought I was set.

Then, halfway between one tiny rural town and the next, I felt the steering wheel wrench in my hand. I slowed down and pulled the car up only to find my tyre had blown out and was completely flat. I reached for my phone only to be confronted by a black screen. In all my haste I hadn't realised my battery was nearly flat, and I didn't have a charger. I felt dread in the pit of my stomach. If I wanted to get moving again, it was going to be up to me.

I opened the boot where the spare tyre was kept and looked for the jack. There it was, sitting in its allotted holder. But there was a problem: the jack handle was missing and it was going to be impossible for me to manage without it. I was starting to feel doubtful that I would make the interview, but I was trying to contain my rising panic.

As I stood there, hands clenched at my side, I resisted the urge to cry. I tried to figure out what to do. Then a ute appeared in the distance, and I held up my hand to get the driver's attention. A man pulled up and rolled down his window.

'Are you okay? Anything I can do?' he asked. I explained my predicament. He got out of his car and walked to my boot, where he reached inside and pulled out the spare tyre.

'No jack handle is the least of your worries,' he said. 'The spare is flat too.'

I couldn't believe it.

'Are you in a hurry?' he asked.

'A bit,' I replied, explaining how I had an important interview and was on a serious deadline.

'I reckon the spare from my wife's car would do the trick,' he offered. 'But it's at my house, and it will take me twenty minutes to get there and back. That okay?' He had been heading in the opposite direction. I was both surprised and touched by his offer.

'No, no, I couldn't ask that of you. That's beyond kind,' I said. 'You've already done so much to try to help me.'

And here is what he said that made me realise how powerful gratitude is.

'It would make me feel even better to know I'd helped you as much as I can,' he said. 'You'd be doing *me* the favour!'

He introduced himself as Harry, and smiled with a genuineness that made me trust him. I was thankful for his assistance, but what really struck me was how grateful he was for the opportunity to help.

He headed off in his ute and, true to his word, returned twenty minutes later with a triumphant look on his face. He changed the tyre and sent me on my way. And I made it just in time for my interview.

This experience taught me so much about the way gratitude can be given and received, and how we can create scenarios in our lives where gratitude can flourish. My rescuer that day didn't need thanks—his desire to help came from a deeper intention to be of service, and he was grateful that I accepted his offer. And what evolved from this exchange was a bond between us— a sense of shared humanity—that exemplified the need we have to help others. Harry clearly felt satisfied that he had been of service. I was full of gratitude for him. He'd given me his details to reimburse him for the spare tyre and I took so much pleasure in sending him a gift voucher for a local restaurant, too. *Forever grateful to you. Enjoy a lovely meal out with your wife on me,* I texted the next day. We shared our gratitude. Everyone felt good. Gratitude truly is one of the fastest ways to happiness.

•

Learning how to feel and express gratitude is an important life skill regardless of your age. There is no rule as to when you can begin a practice of expressing more gratitude—the youngest child is capable of grasping the concept of thankfulness, and we can model this behaviour for them every day. We can also express our own gratitude to young children and teach them what it feels like to be on the receiving end of grace. And we can make a conscious decision to express our gratitude to everyone in our lives—our family members, our friends, our colleagues and the strangers we meet.

Don't forget to express gratitude to yourself, too. There are so many opportunities for us to pause and acknowledge the grace we have shown. This practice adds immeasurably to our sense of self, our confidence, our self-awareness and our consciousness. Building a capacity for gratitude is like working out your muscles: the more you do, the stronger you become and the more obvious the effects are on your body, heart and mind. The act of stopping and noticing, of not taking life for granted, immediately centres us in the present moment. In a life of greatness, being mindful and present to ourselves and others is an essential skill. Something shifts in the way you carry yourself in the world when you live this way; perhaps it is the kindness in your eyes, the softness in your face or the palpable sense of presence and attention you bring to the moment. Grateful people are delightful to be around and, in the best of situations, their gratitude is contagious.

Yes, it can be a challenge to embody gratitude when times are hard. Yet gratitude leads to change: it gives us the chance to reflect on and alter our actions. Gratitude can help us grow and mature, to realise our full potential—and this is fundamental to living a life of greatness. It is deeply connected with our sense of self-love. It helps us develop deeper feelings of relatedness with all living things. It is a remarkably simple practice, yet we often neglect it or find it hard to action in our fast-paced, attention-seeking world. So, the simplest and most effective pathway to gratitude is to first practise slowing down and noticing what is in you and around you that gives you a sense of grace. In a life of greatness there is much to feel thankful for. Remind yourself daily what you're grateful for, and you will find there is always more.

Chapter 12

The freedom in forgiveness

Forgiveness is the fragrance, rare and sweet, that
flowers yield when trampled on by feet.

Ella A. Giles

'It's happened again,' said Jade as she dropped her handbag to the ground. 'I'm going to be so late for work.' Her little blue car was parked exactly where she always left it at night: out the front of the house she shared with her parents on a pretty street in bayside Melbourne. 'This is the third time since Easter,' Jade muttered to herself. She sat on the kerb and tried to gather her composure. Not only was it a huge inconvenience, the cost of having multiple tyres replaced was starting to become a financial drain. *Who has this many flats?* she thought to herself. The first time was just random, the second time seemed a bit unlucky, the third time . . . it seemed improbable. Then she'd lost count.

'In all my years of driving, I've never seen so many flat tyres,' said Jade's dad. 'Something is going on.'

Jade felt a wash of fear in her belly. She was in her late teens, she had great friends, she loved to go out dancing and she had a fabulous job she enjoyed, with a terrific boss. The idea that someone would be deliberately targeting her—it didn't make sense.

When Jade first told me her story, many years later, I was shocked. Jade and I had been friends for years, decades even, and I hadn't had an inkling of what had been going on for her back then. We'd first met when we were both fifteen and students in the same drama class. Over the years our lives had drifted in different directions, but we always found time to catch up and hear about each other's lives. This story was unexpected—it was the kind of thing that happened to 'other' people, not your own friends.

We were sitting on the balcony of a seaside cafe sharing lunch, chatting about a recent challenge I had gone through, when a simple question emerged: 'Have you ever had to forgive someone and it was hard?' This opened up a profound story about Jade's life. As she told it, I felt a mixture of disbelief and admiration for her courage and wisdom.

'Let's document this,' Jade's dad had said. 'Build a picture of the dates. I think we need to let the police know, too.'

Over the next few weeks, with the help of the police, Jade built up a timeline of all the punctures that had happened. Thirteen.

Thirteen incidents over a period of six months. This was no coincidence.

'Jade, we think you are being purposely targeted,' said the local police officer as they reviewed the list. 'These are not punctures, these are slashes.'

Then the letter arrived at work. A handwritten note in block-style letters—the type of handwriting taught in schools decades ago. When Jade arrived at the office that morning, her manager Liz took her aside.

'Sit down. I don't want you to be alarmed, but something arrived in the mail today and I need to show it to you,' said Liz.

Liz read the contents of the letter out loud: *Hi, you employ a Scandinavian girl by the name of Jade, and she works at your head office and when she's not at your premises, she is one of the biggest prostitutes we know. She operates full-time from a brothel in eastern Melbourne.*

'I'm not a prostitute!' said Jade. 'Who sent that?'

'I know that,' said Liz. 'You've never got any money,' she joked. But then her face grew serious and she said, 'It has no sign-off. Is everything okay?'

'I don't know what is happening', said Jade, 'but I think I need to take this to the police.'

The police officer took a considered look at the letter and said, 'Jade, we believe you are the victim of a stalker. Do you have any idea who it could be?'

The handwriting indicated it was an older man. Jade didn't know any elderly men except her grandpa, who'd already passed away, and Bill, her neighbour.

'In 80 per cent of stalking cases it is someone known to the victim,' said the police officer. 'Could it be Bill?'

Jade's mind went into overdrive. Bill was almost 80 years old and had moved in next door about a year earlier. He was friendly—perhaps overly friendly, Jade now thought. Jade had been kind, but kept her chats with him short. He popped over a lot and sometimes he mowed their lawns without asking. That had been a bit weird, but the family had accepted it as a nice gesture from a neighbour.

Jade realised that Bill always seemed to be about. When she got back from work, he'd be out hosing his lawn. When she arrived home from a night out dancing, even if it was 5 a.m., he was out the front of his house. Jade assumed he was an early riser. But her discomfort was now growing.

Jade recalled that Bill had asked her mum when she'd be home from work many times. He had brought golf balls over for her dad when he wasn't there. Actually, he never came over when her dad was home.

The day Jade figured out her stalker was probably Bill, a friend had dropped by to pick her up to go and see a movie. In the time it took for her friend to come inside and say hello, her tyres had been slashed too.

'He knows all your moves with precision,' the police officer said. 'He knows when to be there. We don't have what we need to make an arrest yet. But we believe in these situations he will be looking for windows of opportunity. Be careful.'

Jade felt chilled to the core. They couldn't prove it yet, but she knew it deep down. Then something else happened. Just a few days later, while driving, she lost control of her car and ended up on the nature strip of a busy road. It turned out that two metal poles had been wedged diagonally under her car axles. As she had driven, one had become dislodged and it had jammed on the bitumen before piercing through the floor of her car, narrowly missing her. Fortunately the sound of metal on bitumen had made her slow down.

That afternoon the police set up a neighbourhood door knock regarding the car vandalism in Jade's street. How Bill reacted to the news of the surveillance plan they were going to implement would hopefully give probable cause for a warrant.

Bill's reaction was just what they needed. 'Are you accusing me?' he demanded in a high voice.

The police told him no, but they had enough to get a warrant for handwriting samples from Bill that could be matched to the horrible letter sent to Jade's work. They got the samples and then, before they were able to interview Bill, he confessed.

Jade's family moved away from the street immediately and started life again in a new and more private house. But it affected everyone, especially Jade. Her ordeal was not over yet—it wouldn't be over for a long time, and not until she could practise the art of forgiveness.

Jade was never able to understand why she was Bill's target. Sometimes Bill had commented that she reminded him of his wife. If his motivation was to keep Jade at home and afraid, he succeeded—for the next five years, even when she had moved again and was living in a share house with friends, Jade was constantly on guard. If there was a gap between the bottom of the venetian blinds and the windowsill she would stuff it with towels so no one could see in. For years she undressed under the covers of her bed. She felt too paralysed to change anything, and this wasn't helped by the fact that, due to Bill's age and his poor mental and physical health, any charges she pressed were unlikely to amount to anything. She was angry that there had been no retribution or justice for her. Bill had written her an apology letter, but it had done little to quell her anxieties. Years later, he was still affecting how she was living. By her own account, it was insanity.

One day, as Jade was under her doona changing into her red bikini for a pool party at her own home, she had a moment. She realised it was ridiculous to still be suffering in this way, and from then she set about changing it. She realised she could not move forward in life if she was stuck in this energy that kept her paralysed. That day she made a conscious decision to forgive Bill. It was a decision that she has continued to make every day since.

Having a strong mind and capacity for inner reflection was one of Jade's superpowers, and she used this to her advantage. She realised that the likelihood of being stalked again was remote, and that she was never alone, and never stuck. She said to herself, 'I am not going to live in fear of this. I have to get over it.' It sounded harsh, but it helped her release Bill and the events that had transpired. She started to live normally again. Eventually she got to a point where she wasn't thinking about him anymore. Forgiveness was the key.

It was the release of Bill from her mind that set Jade free. In acting from a space of forgiveness she was no longer captive to him. Holding on to the horror had only confined her more. She did not wish ill will on anyone, and she believed karma would take care of it.

Forgiveness has been potent for Jade, but it took time. Once she realised she was the only one keeping herself captive, she knew forgiveness meant freedom. Not forgiving had created more of the same pain. The saying 'Take away the audience and the actor has no stage' was something Jade and I had learnt in drama school, and it had informed many aspects of her life— including pointing her to the power of forgiveness. But one of Jade's most profound insights was this: 'What he did to me, I was then doing to myself—until I could find forgiveness.'

Jade decided her life was not going to be defined by this experience, and she flourished.

•

Forgiveness does not have to mean condoning what happened. Rather, it is a way to take the power back into your life and move forward, especially when you are feeling stuck. It's difficult to actualise our full potential if we remain stuck in past hurts. There is truth in the statement that hatred never ends hatred. It is important that we tend to our suffering with loving kindness.

One way we can tap into the compassion in our hearts is to imagine the person who we feel has wronged us as a child. This allows space in our psyches to see that person as a human who is still learning and making mistakes.

Forgiveness takes courage. The *Bhagavad Gita* says, 'If you want to see the brave, look to those who can return love for hatred. If you want to see the heroic, look to those who can forgive.'

While forgiveness does not mean you forget, it does mean you recognise suffering and do all you can to prevent that suffering from happening again. It is not a passive action but an act of courage that sees you standing up for what matters. You do everything you can to stand in the way of someone else experiencing harm. It is a slow and patient process that takes as long as it takes. It is ultimately about putting down the burden of hatred from the past and living with care and joy. Forgiveness is for *you*.

There is a fable about two former prisoners of war who reunited 25 years after the war ended. They had both suffered terrible atrocities during wartime. The first man asked the other, 'Have you forgiven your captors yet?' When his friend answered, 'No, never', the first man replied, 'Then they still have you in prison, don't they? You're not free.'

There are many people whose actions we may consider unforgivable. If ever there were reason to lack the capacity for forgiveness, a mass murder in which your child was killed would surely be one. Scarlett Lewis, whose six-year-old son Jesse was murdered during the Sandy Hook Elementary School massacre in Connecticut in 2012, shared her heart-wrenching story of forgiveness with me on *A Life of Greatness*. Scarlett chose love and forgiveness, rather than anger and resentment, as a way to heal. Her ongoing gift to the world is the Jesse Lewis Choose Love Movement, which works to create safer and more loving communities and spread compassion and forgiveness throughout the world.

As the tenth anniversary of the horrific event passed, Scarlett reflected on the profound and enduring legacy of her son's life. She told me how forgiveness has helped her transform her pain into a meaningful contribution to the world. Scarlett opened her heart and was able to forgive the shooter, Adam Lanza, who was twenty years old at the time of the incident. She made no excuses for him, but through her grieving came to an important realisation: that the societal limitations causing Adam to be so full of suffering were everyone's responsibility—even hers.

This set her on a pathway of understanding the power of forgiveness. She embraced Jesse's enduring message of 'nurturing healing love': three words the young boy had written on their kitchen chalkboard shortly before his passing. 'I thought I would dissolve in grief,' Scarlett told me, 'but Jesse's words were a message of how to be. I realised living his message was part of the purpose I was supposed to live.'

To Scarlett, these three words carried a simple but deeply affecting message: nurturing meant loving kindness and gratitude; healing meant forgiveness; love was compassion in action. Jesse left an indelible mark on the lives of those who loved him. Scarlett now describes forgiveness as choosing to let go of anger and resentment towards yourself or someone else, to surrender thoughts of revenge and to move forward with your personal power intact.

Jesse was also a hero that day. He managed to save nine other children by ushering them out of the room while the shooter was distracted. 'He courageously put others before himself that day, and I knew I had to be the best version of myself too, even in grief, and certainly beyond that,' she said. 'Yes, I was sad and angry, but I also had purpose and direction, and these incredible signs he was with me.'

Scarlett decided she was not going to be another one of the shooter's victims. Instead she became part of the solution by taking positive action. 'When I chose forgiveness, I was able to step outside of my own pain to help other people,' she said. Through the Choose Love Movement, Scarlett teaches people to grow and transform through their challenges. She believes the work she is doing helps and heals young people so they don't feel so disconnected that committing murder in a school seems like their only option. 'Service was a part of my healing, and I found a way to choose love and compassion,' she said.

Scarlett believes that when Charles Darwin talked about survival of the fittest, what he actually meant was survival of the most sympathetic, the most altruistic and the most compassionate. 'Society thrives through compassion and forgiveness,' she told me. 'This is how we get better. This is how we flourish.'

I asked Scarlett what she wanted everyone to remember in Jesse's honour. She said, 'We have the power to always choose love and forgiveness—every time.' Without forgiveness, life may have been unbearable for Scarlett, and many others.

•

Research indicates how powerful forgiveness is in reducing suffering and bringing greater happiness, dignity and harmony to our lives. It increases our capacity to deal with emotional challenges, supports us to have healthier relationships, reduces symptoms of depression and anxiety, improves self-esteem and has a positive impact on our physical and general health.[9] Letting go of bitterness can lower our blood pressure, improve our heart health and increase our immune system strength.

There is no downside to forgiveness. Thoughts of goodwill towards another person helps us feel better. Forgiveness does not ask us to excuse the other's actions but to let go of what isn't serving us. We free up important real estate in our minds that we can use to reach our full potential. And we heal.

Former National Rugby League (NRL) superstar Alex McKinnon shared his powerful story of healing and letting go when I interviewed him on my podcast. He was just 22 years old when life delivered him a crushing blow. During a dynamic rugby game at Melbourne's AAMI Park he was tackled to the ground. He describes being lifted up with his arms pinned to his side. As he tried to duck, he hit the ground at an angle. He remembers the eerie silence of 25,000 shocked fans as he lay on the turf. The angle of the impact caused him to suffer a spinal cord injury, specifically fractures to his C4 and C5 vertebrae. Alex was made a quadriplegic that day. The rugby career he had invested in since age five, and the achievements he still had in front of him, suddenly evaporated—along with his sense of identity.

Alex spent the next year in hospitals and rehabilitation centres learning to live a completely new life. 'Life was so busy with appointments that I barely had a chance to think. Nothing had really sunk in,' he said. 'But then after that first year I moved back to Newcastle, close to where I had grown up, and things started to hit home. I couldn't work, I couldn't drive. I was alone a lot, and I had time to think.'

In that period, Alex carried anger, hatred and resentment towards the player who had tackled him, and the rest of the team. He hadn't spoken to anyone about how he was feeling.

'I was trying to adapt to life as a quadriplegic and for months I just sat in that pain. And that's when all of my emotions came up.'

Alex realised, in a moment of truth, that the only way he could truly recover would be to move towards forgiveness. Aware that the eyes of his family, his friends and his fans were on him, he decided to make changes in his life so he could demonstrate true leadership.

He began by speaking to the opposing team's captain, who had made some comments after the event that Alex had found tough. 'He didn't understand the enormity of his words or actions,' said Alex. 'I told him I forgave him.'

Then Alex had another conversation, in which he expressed his forgiveness to the player who had tackled him. 'There were things

I needed to get off my chest. I realised he didn't intentionally set about putting me in a wheelchair. These conversations set me free.'

Alex described the immediate feeling of relief that overcame him, and what a massive turning point these conversations were in his life. Forgiveness had lifted a heavy burden from him.

For Alex, forgiveness was not optional: it was an essential step in reshaping his life. When people ask him how he moved past such a life-changing injury, he tells them he had to decide what he wanted and act on it. He decided to stop being self-absorbed and take a step forward—to find new purpose in his life and approach it in a different way. Forgiveness gave him the space to get to know himself and take positive actions to step forward on his own terms. His view of life was transformed.

Today Alex no longer asks, 'Why me?' In fact, he says he wouldn't change a thing in his life. 'I honestly feel so lucky I have experienced what I've been through. I've met people I wouldn't have met, and I'm doing things I would have never imagined for myself.' Ten years on, Alex is studying psychology at university and has three beautiful daughters.

'Yes, some things are still tough but that's life. Life had tough times before my injury. We can't avoid that. But I've learnt it's about the process, not the outcome.' Alex feels a sense of gratitude for how his injury opened up a different world to him. Forgiveness kicked open the door.

•

The freedom in forgiveness

There are so many incredible stories of forgiveness in the world and across history. As Jesus died on the cross, his last words were, 'Father, forgive them, for they do not know what they are doing.' There are many situations in which it might feel unfathomable to offer forgiveness to another. Yet forgiveness doesn't mean you have to engage further with that person. It simply means you defuse the pain that, if left to fester, would only add to your own misery and discomfort. It's okay to say things are not okay; the real freedom is in taking action and making conscious choices to reduce your suffering.

Offering forgiveness can be an inner practice as much as an outer practice. It is also okay to take your time. Forgiveness is serious business, and if it is not the right time yet, honour that and give yourself space to feel into the emotions further. Forgiveness isn't about steamrolling your emotions or wishing them away. The truth of forgiveness is that it needs to be felt at a gut level, and by your whole heart. Words of forgiveness are powerful, but they need to be spoken with true intent.

If you have experienced traumatic events, forgiveness may only be possible after healing has occurred on multiple levels: body, mind and heart. The act of forgiveness may take many years. It may be a gradual process of stripping back layers and layers of pain. Bring all the compassion you can muster to yourself, and remember your innate loving heart.

There will always be sorrows in life. People will aggrieve us, let us down, steal from us or hurt us or our loved ones. The choice to make every day is to live in love and focus on our capacity for renewal by letting go. Forgiveness helps us embrace a life of greatness because it frees us from the past and lets us focus our energies on the potential of our future. We can choose not to pass our sorrows on to others. We can choose to take our power back and heal from our pain. We can choose to be all we can be.

Forgiveness is ultimately for the forgiver.

Chapter 13

Finding your people

Friends . . . they cherish one another's hopes. They are kind to one another's dreams.

Henry David Thoreau

Finding time to nurture our friendships is one of the best ways to live a life of greatness. Biologically and psychologically, we need the fulfilment of friendships. Connecting with our people helps build our sense of identity and belonging in the world. Good friends support us to reach our full potential. Adult life is full of demands that typically aren't part of childhood, but the need for solid and supportive friendships is just as real as it was back then.

Even if you only have a handful of good friends, you are nailing life. I have found that it's not about the number of friends you have but the quality of those friendships. When we're growing up we may find ourselves forced into social circles that are not in full alignment with who we are or what we value most. As adults we can be more discerning. We can choose to align ourselves with people who are more like-minded. And most of us don't have buckets of time to invest in friendships; we might have families, jobs, homes and all manner of commitments and demands. This means the decisions we make about who we choose to share time with matter. When our time is precious, so too are our friendships.

I have seen changes in my friendships as I have grown and matured. Some friendships have faded or dropped away organically. Others have lingered and some have prospered. Some people feel that it's harder to make new friends in adulthood, while many find that it's easier. When you are being true to yourself and living in a purposeful way, you tend to attract others who you feel an instant connection with. These friendships based on shared values have the capacity to be extremely meaningful.

I have become careful about who I let into my inner friendship circle as I've become older. I am more aware of the influences I have in my life and protective of the peace I have managed to cultivate. I have values that I aspire to live by, and I need to see those values reflected in who I associate with. There's plenty of research suggesting that the company we keep shapes our experience of the world. If we are around achievement-orientated, expansionary types of people, this will also become our experience. If we spend a lot of time with people who have more negative thought patterns, we may take these on as part of our reality. One study found that the presence of a friend actually changed how people viewed the steepness of a hill.[10] With a friend by their side, research participants assessed the hill as being less steep than when they were alone. Social support affected how they perceived the challenge level of the hill, and how they evaluated their ability to master it. Having a friend there meant they were more likely to try to walk or run up the hill, and they were more likely to make it to the top. We could consider the task of getting up a hill as a metaphor for the many challenges and stressors we encounter in life. The support of a friend may mean you try things that alone you might avoid.

The 'group think' of the people you associate with has a powerful pull. Your people should be nourishing, positive forces who help you flourish in your life of greatness rather than shy away or suffer from dis-ease.

Our need for friendship, community, connection, love and touch is hardwired into our biology.[11] Our brains have evolved to support complex social lives. From the time we are born and perhaps even before, our brain circuitry develops as a multi-faceted system designed for empathy, cooperation, love and sharing. We are wired to care, and we subconsciously know that other people provide us with safety and increase our ability to achieve. When we experience social touch via a stroke of the skin, for example, neural pathways are activated that facilitate bonding. Our behaviour and biology will mimic that of significant others from birth. Even our heart rates will sync.

Friendships can have a profound impact on our health and wellbeing. Research shows that people with friends are less likely to die from all causes including heart disease and a range of chronic illnesses.[12] We deal with life differently when we have friends, and this lowers our heart's reactivity to stress and other challenges. Having friends protects against stress and helps prevent mental health issues such as depression and anxiety.[13] Any type of social interaction can be beneficial, so it can be just as valuable to interact with strangers as it is to build strong social connections with friends and family members. Simply put, loneliness is detrimental to health, and social isolation can lead to premature death.

Nourishing friendships increase happiness, improve your sense of belonging and purpose and increase your self-confidence and self-worth. Think about a time when you've had a huge day at work or with the kids, and a friend has been a form of salvation at the end of the day. It is our closest friends, our people, who are also there for us when we need them most, especially when things are not going well. Life is full of challenges and traumas, even when we are on the path to greatness. When we experience the loss of loved ones, job changes, relationship breakdowns and illnesses, real friends are there to support us through it all.

The positive effects of friendship can be measured in terms of longevity, too. The world's longest-living people tend to have close friends and strong social networks.[14]

As I have become more discerning about the friendships I nourish in my life, I have found myself forming deeper and more fruitful connections. I focus on the qualities of friendship I most want to invite into my life. What makes a good friend will be different for everyone, but the best connections grow in the presence of trust, vulnerability, authenticity and loyalty.

I've also found that like attracts like, and this encourages me to turn the lens back on myself and consider what I bring to my friendships. It's really simple: you need to be the friend you seek. It's worth thinking about what matters most to you and whether you are radiating those qualities yourself. You might also discover what it takes to be your own best friend. This is connected to finding your own sense of authenticity, and will help you meet people who are growing in a similar direction. That's how you find your people.

We've all experienced a draining friendship and understand how challenging—and damaging—that can be. As you embrace a life of greatness, there may be some friendships that don't survive your transition. Be comforted by the simple notion that friendships exist for a season, a reason or a lifetime. Some friendships have timeframes and that is okay. Our task is to let go with grace and loving kindness. It is okay to decide a friendship isn't for you and isn't aligned with who you are now. Likewise, everyone you meet has a different life path and will go through changes over time. This can be tough if you're holding on to the belief that friendships should last forever. It's simply not true. Sometimes friendships fade. Adults can sometimes make the world unnecessarily complex and demanding, particularly when it comes to friends.

•

My twelve-year-old son Oliver has taught me so many things about friendship. He sees everyone as equal, and he lives this every day: his teachers tell me he is always the first one to invite the new kid at school into a game.

One day I was in the kitchen preparing sandwiches for Oliver and the friend he had invited over to hang out. The front gate had barely clicked open and Oliver, who had been watching TV in the living room, had jumped to his feet. His face beamed with excitement. His energy was alive.

'He's here, he's here,' he chanted. 'Jake's here.'

Our old-fashioned, heavy silver door knocker rapped with an energy to match Oliver's. Bright light flooded the hallway as the door was flung open and there, silhouetted in the morning light, was Jake, dressed in his favourite soccer jersey. Oliver ran towards him and they embraced quickly. I was touched by the simple joy they had in seeing one another. The boys disappeared into the living room and I was left to say goodbye to Jake's dad.

'They'll have a great time,' I said, and we nodded in unison. A fun-filled 24 hours lay ahead of them: movies, bike riding, soccer and pizza to celebrate the end of term. We already knew there wouldn't be a single issue. The relationship between our sons had all the hallmarks of a quality friendship, of acceptance and non-judgement. And they had so much fun together.

'Jake is a gorgeous boy,' I said. 'I love how those two never have a bad word to say about one another.' It was true. Despite all sorts of changes in the years they had been friends, they had always celebrated one another. Their friendship was beautiful to witness because they accepted each other's qualities and quirks. There was an innocence and purity to their relationship—a simplicity that perhaps some adults would see as naive, but I have always thought a sign of great wisdom. These are friendship qualities we can also strive to capture as adults.

Later, whoops of glee flooded into the house from the back garden as the boys kicked a soccer ball between some makeshift goalposts. Soccer was a formidable glue in their relationship, one that had grown with them since kindergarten. Shared passions, clear communication, conquering the universe—they had it all. I realise there are children (and adults) who find it hard to foster friendships for all sorts of reasons, and there are people who simply prefer their own company. I have never taken friendship for granted. I know that even in the best connections there can be sources of conflict. Resolving this conflict is one of life's great skills. Oliver has a natural affinity with people. He is a peace-seeker. He welcomes people in. It is simply enough that he likes them—that makes them okay. He genuinely cares for and respects his friends, and it seems that other kids gravitate towards him.

I watched the boys from the doorway for a few more minutes as they kicked the ball to one another. They'd found their people when they found each other. It's no different for us grown-ups.

•

When my friend Hannah first met Simon in primary school, she thought they would be lifelong friends. For years they grew together, best friends who shared every experience and had much in common. Platonic in nature, their friendship endured the typical stages of teenagerhood as love interests came and went. Through everything their bond only strengthened. To Hannah, Simon felt more like a brother than her own siblings, and there was nothing she couldn't or wouldn't tell him. They shopped together for hours and listened to the same music while they talked about their relationships, school and life. They rarely argued. They shared a passion for the party life and dancing long after high school ended.

Hannah and Simon had made a pact that if they weren't partnered with other people by the time they turned 30, they would marry and love each other's company forever. It was hard to imagine anything separating them. They had spent decades together.

We probably all relate to that expansive feeling that defines our high-school friendships. They are the locus of our world. But life changes, we change, and what once felt like a non-negotiable can one day feel untenable. That's how Hannah describes the end of the friendship, which wasn't so much an abrupt halt as a slow fade. Perhaps, she reflects, it would have been easier if they'd had a falling-out and vowed never to talk again, but it wasn't like that. What had bonded them together, a love for partying, no longer mattered to her. 'I just didn't feel a synergy there anymore,' she told me. 'I wanted different things in my life, and I knew I didn't want to be doing the same thing over and over again.'

One of the most challenging things Hannah was left to reconcile was the empty space in her life. She remembers one day, sitting around a dinner table with her old crew, realising she felt terribly out of place. Simon was part of that group too, and even with him Hannah felt a strangeness.

Hannah knows it is rare for anyone to hold on to high-school friendships forever, but in her heart she always thought she would be the exception—the person who had the same friends for all time. What she didn't factor in was her own evolution.

What gave her solace, even through the feelings of pain and loss, was realising that people come into your life for seasons. When you meet someone, you're both in a particular season of life. Sometimes those seasons align, sometimes they don't. Hannah had simply entered a new season in her life, and Simon no longer fit.

Hannah arrived at an understanding that friendships can become memories, and you can't hold on too tight to people. There is a freedom in accepting that sometimes you're not meant to be friends anymore, and that's okay. One of the most effective strategies she has learnt is to simply send the friend off in love.

Hannah is now much more aware of her own energy and has learnt how much each person has to contribute to keep friendships alive. 'If you are constantly the one calling, it becomes not only disheartening, but also unsustainable,' she said. Friendships have to be reciprocal—there is mutual obligation in real friendships. You also need to be able to establish strong boundaries. Friends who can't respect your boundaries will naturally fall away. Over time we become much better at understanding how different friendships serve us. We realise it is almost impossible to have a real friendship with someone who can't see beyond their own needs. We also learn it is wise to carefully remove ourselves from potentially harmful friendships with people who don't show up or value being in reciprocity, because it is impossible for friendships such as these to contribute to our life of greatness. Some people simply don't, can't or won't change. 'If you observe a friend directing shitty behaviour towards another person, you have to accept that you won't be immune to that behaviour—you will get it too, eventually,' Hannah reflected.

The friendships worth cultivating provide healing and joy. These friends are people who are doing the work—who own who they are and live from a place of truth and integrity. The greatest friends are able to be honest when it matters. They are the friends who notice things are off before things veer off course. Trust that. Conversely, when you're doing the work yourself, you are more awake to other people's behaviours and motivations. Many people live unaware of how they are showing up, and it's our choice how much we invest in these connections.

When friendships fade, this is your chance for self-reflection. Can you attend to those things in yourself that need your love? Caring for yourself in these times gives you the space to accept that friendships end—it's not wrong, it's not personal, it's just what it is. Hannah definitely missed Simon. But when those feelings became overwhelming she tried to picture herself in her old way of being with him, and quickly realised she didn't want that after all—in fact, she felt quite repulsed by the idea. She saw how much we can romanticise past relationships with nostalgia. It's a relief sometimes to realise what you are yearning for isn't even reality.

Hannah also realised her personal values—integrity, showing up, authenticity and clear and direct communication—had always guided her. Like Hannah, you will notice immediately when your values are not shared by other people—their behaviour jars on you. Be clear in what you will accept in your life. You can't change someone's values but you do have capacity for acceptance, to let them go in grace. 'Just keep sending love' is a mantra that truly works in these circumstances.

Great friendship is not about 'time served'. New friends can arrive in your life at any time. Some of my deepest connections have begun in recent years and have been quick to flourish. Today I am blessed with people I call soul friends—my inner circle, the people who see me and greatly enrich my life. I call them soul friends because they feel like home. I feel genuine love for them and I feel this love flowing back to me.

When you find your people, you hold a sacred position in their lives. Honour this. Nurture your friends in all the ways you can, especially with your time and your listening. Be there for them. Support them through major life events and crises, and be there through their happiness and joy. Hold their stories and their secrets, their vulnerability and safety.

Our friendships should lift us up. They should be alive with mutuality and reciprocity, and help us reach our full potential. My dearest friends and I often connect in this way. The simple act of reaching out and letting people know you are thinking about them can be a beautiful way to honour friendships in the moment. And it goes both ways. A message will pop up in my inbox at random times of the day. *Love you Sar, have a great day, J xx.* Just a few words, letting me know I am in someone's thoughts. I am grateful for those friends. We value each other and it is delightfully uncomplicated.

The best friendships are based on a shared understanding of the need to collaborate and not compete. Just like Oliver and his friend Jake have taught me, celebrating each other is key to connection.

True friends will always build you up. They will be steadfast and celebrate you and your path towards greatness. They will encourage you in your endeavours and hold you accountable. And they will always be honest (with kindness). That is how you grow; that is where real fulfilment in friendship lies. And that's why I cherish my friendship with Hannah.

The energy of a great friendship will give your life forward momentum. Your friends will show you possibilities you may not have considered before. Great friendships require your attention but are not draining. Your effort fuels increasingly deeper connections and greater vulnerability. These friendships are safe places to show up in all your insecurities and be seen, met and supported. Your people should be among your primary support systems. If this is not the case—if you can't ask to be held in a vulnerable space—think about where your time and capacity for love and connection could be better shared.

You deserve to have good friendships. When you find friends you can call your people, hold on to them.

Chapter 14

The power of your breath

When the breath is unsteady all is unsteady. When the breath is still, all is still.

Svātmārāma

I was seated in the aisle, the seat I had requested when I booked. I had my seatbelt fastened and my tray table stowed. Around me I heard the arhythmic clicks as other passengers fastened their seatbelts or slammed the overhead lockers shut. There was a lot of noise—and many distractions—but it wasn't really helping me. I was too hot one minute and chilly the next. I crossed my arms and immediately felt uncomfortable. I clasped my hands together in my lap and stared at my fingernails. I grasped the armrest so tight my knuckles went white. The flight attendant had told us all what to do in the unlikely situation of a midair incident. That didn't help either.

I am a nervous flyer. I've been that way for most of my adult life. I have never had anything happen on a flight to make me fearful—there is no story as to why I am like this. I'd tried a few different strategies—desensitisation therapy, distraction techniques and hypnotherapy-style interventions—to try to overcome my discomfort. My fear stemmed from the feeling of entrapment that overrode my ability to be calm. I knew that once I was in the air, there was no getting off. I coped with take-off and landing well enough, but it was the claustrophobic feel of the cabin during the flight that turned my insides to jelly. It was something all the rational mind processes in the world couldn't shift. I was better when I had someone flying with me—flying alone had become a real trial—but I still wasn't great. When I started to feel the anxiety rising in me days before flying—not just when I was on the plane—I realised I had to do something more to help myself.

It had all come to a crashing halt one morning as I was preparing for a beach holiday with my family. What should have been a joyful lead-up was turning me inside out. Instead of enjoying the rapidly building excitement my children were feeling, I was shaking so much I had to shut the bedroom door and wrestle with my trembling hands.

'You okay? What's going on, Sarah?' My husband had quietly opened the door and was peeking through the crack.

'I'm feeling really nervous,' I replied.

'The flight?' he asked as he came in and sat down beside me. How well he knew me.

'I think so. I want to be excited with the children, but I can't get past this feeling.'

'I know I can tell you it's all going to be okay—and I know you know that,' he said. We sat silently side-by-side on the bed as the sound of our children giggling with excitement filtered down the hallway. And of course the clock was ticking. I needed to gather myself. We had to get to the airport and make our flight.

Then my husband said something so simple yet so insightful. 'Why don't you try some breathwork? Maybe the box technique?'

'Right now?' I asked.

'Take ten minutes,' he said.

He was right, of course. This simple suggestion proved to be the beginning of an enormous change for me. With my husband and the children by my side I took the first steps—the first breaths—towards overcoming my fear. And we had a brilliant holiday.

The next time I was scheduled to fly alone for an interstate meeting, my husband's words rang in my ears. I arrived at the airport with plenty of time to make my flight—in the past I would often get there at the last minute as a way to control my rising panic—and I made a commitment to myself to be 100 per cent aware of what my body was doing and how I was responding.

I felt my heartbeat quicken at the boarding gate, and instead of trying to talk myself out of my feelings, I let them be. I acknowledged I was on edge and didn't try to change it. Immediately my body responded with a few deeper breaths. It was like my breath wanted to help me, that it was really there for me. This was a new awareness for me. My breath was showing me the way.

As I walked up the boarding stairs to the aircraft I kept my breath front of mind. I consciously took a deep breath in for four counts, held it for four counts, and consciously let it out for four counts before holding for another four counts. This type of breathing, which my husband had taught me—box breathing—was the simplest and most direct way I'd found to focus on my breath in the moment. And as my breath steadied, so did my heartbeat. When my heart calmed, my anxiety was soothed also. I felt the immediate link between what I was doing and how I was feeling. You might think this is breathing 101—in breath, hold, out breath, hold—but you might also be surprised how messy our breathing can be when we don't focus on it. Stop right now and check in on yours. Take a breath—a full conscious breath—and feel the difference.

After a few minutes waiting in line (and breathing) I got to my seat and fastened my seatbelt. This was the moment when my panic usually went into overdrive, but this time I was ready. Breathe in for four, hold for four, breathe out for four, hold for four—long and slow, over and over again. I closed my eyes and let the sound of my breath overwhelm my senses. My heart felt soft and steady, my hands were relaxed. My whole body felt different to how it had felt the last time I'd flown: it was alive and ready but receptive and relaxed. This was a new way for me to be.

That day, on that flight, breath helped me transform my fears. And from that moment on, it was permanent. I had tools that really worked. Over time, the more I flew the less anxiety I felt. Breathing had worked when nothing else had, and today I can fly anywhere—even a long-haul flight to the other side of the world—without fear. I've taught this method to people I coach who have anxiety, as well as people with flying phobias, and they have all enjoyed positive outcomes. Breath was a drug-free solution that was always in me. It showed me I had the power to regulate my nervous system. Breath is a miracle. When we harness its potential it can do so much for us.

•

The first thing we do in life—the very first thing that says we are here—is take a breath. At the end of our lives the same thing is true. We draw our last breath as life leaves our body, and this is the sign that we have passed. Breathing is a highly symbolic act that marks a beginning and an end, and yet it is present in our everyday as a series of beginnings and endings that occur repeatedly, unconsciously and reliably, providing our bodies with the vital oxygen they need to stay alive. It is remarkable then that we often go through life without paying much attention to our breath. We take breathing for granted, expecting it to always be there—and for the most part it is. We are aware of when we are holding our breath in fear, or we feel out of breath due to physical exertion. We may find a view breathtaking, or talk about being breathless in anticipation of something, but it is less common that we talk about the power of the breath, or what being conscious of the breath can do for us.

Practising mindfulness or yoga will bring us into a deeper connection with the breath. The goal with both of these practices is to be increasingly present to breath as a resource that can support us in day-to-day life. I have found this to be a skill and a philosophy that can be incredibly supportive in the pursuit of a conscious life. Breath is one of the most democratic resources available. It is in everyone, it is free, and it is something that we can access at will. Breath unites us across cultures and underscores what it is to be human. Perhaps this is why so many ancient traditions incorporate breathwork into their spiritual and daily practices. The ancient yogic traditions are based on the concept of pranayama—the practice of breath regulation—and ancient texts such as the *Bhagavad Gita* explain how breath control can foster spiritual growth. Mindfulness meditation begins with the breath. Today there is an evolving understanding that breath, and breathwork, has much to offer us in the modern context.

The power of your breath

So how can we use the power of breath to help create a life of greatness? That's what I asked James Nestor, scientific journalist and author of *Breath: The new science of a lost art*, when I interviewed him for *A Life of Greatness*. James's curiosity around breath started with his own health challenges. When a doctor suggested he try breathing classes to help him with some respiratory issues he was having, he noted how much more far-reaching the benefits were than just improved breathing. His experiences with the breath seemed to lack any real explanation, so he embarked on a research project, which also saw him participate in a life-changing experiment. For ten days he lived with his nose obstructed so that he could only breathe through his mouth. Just a few hours into the experiment, during which his vital signs were monitored, his blood pressure shot through the roof—it was higher than it had ever been before. That first night he snored for the first time ever, and by his account it was a truly awful sleep. Four nights later his snoring had progressed so much that he hit four hours of snore time, and he experienced sleep apnea. Mouth breathing wasn't fun. And here's the thing: most of us are mouth breathers.

After the initial ten days, James reversed the experiment and spent another ten days breathing through his nose. His blood pressure dropped back to normal, his anxiety was gone, his snoring disappeared and all signs of sleep apnoea reduced after three days. His experiment gave him a firsthand understanding of the importance of breathing properly and its health benefits. He found that when we don't breathe properly—in through the nose, out through the mouth—damage starts in the body almost immediately. In his research James also suggested that lifespan increases when we breathe properly, because lung capacity and respiratory health are clear indicators of longevity. Even if we eat the right foods and exercise, he argued, breath is still a greater determinant of longevity. Our bodies want to be in balance and breath is the quickest way there. Breath is an anchor in the body.

James also shared why nasal breathing is so superior to mouth breathing. Nasal breathing ensures the air we take in is filtered and conditioned. Nasal breathing heats or cools air as it enters our body for optimal oxygenation. He shared how, in his research, he looked at skulls from different periods in history, examining specimens from thousands of years ago and comparing them to more recent examples. He observed actual physical changes in the human skull that have been shaped by our recent (he suggests the last 200 years) move to mouth breathing. He observed that modern skulls have smaller mouths, and more crooked teeth. This has altered how we breathe. But we can change that. We can relearn how to breathe and experience the power and benefits of that immediately.

•

The power of your breath

My friend Sam was one of the first people to teach me about the power of my own breath. I met him at the Wim Hof retreat my friend Endi had taken me to, where I faced my fear of the cold through ice bathing—Sam, as the program facilitator, also taught us about breath and how it can be harnessed. He presented us with a range of methods, all backed by scientific evidence, that helped us learn when and how to use the breath with awareness and purpose. I had been practising some breathwork at home, including the method that had helped me overcome my fear of flying, but my first experience of a formal led breathwork process with Sam gave me profound insights into my inner world. It showed me just how entwined breath is with our emotional, physical, spiritual and mental states of being. I have been hooked ever since—because it works.

Sam started by having us lie back on our yoga mats with our eyes closed. I had pulled my hoodie right up over my head, creating a tiny cocoon for myself. To be honest I was a little nervous. This was new to me, and I was very aware it was a preparation activity for the ice bath the next day.

Sam explained the basics of breathing and brain chemistry and described the link between breathing states and the body's production of dimethyltryptamine (DMT), a compound that occurs naturally in plants and animals and that supports non-ordinary states of consciousness and higher levels of thinking.

'Our bodies may have different reactions,' Sam said, 'but just let yourself go and try not to hold on too tightly. You are safe and nothing bad will happen to you.'

I stifled a laugh, another sign of my nerves. I don't find it easy to let go. Control gives me a sense of agency. Now I was about to let it all go, and I wasn't sure what would exist in its place.

Let yourself go, I repeated in my head. I had never been one of those people who could do trust exercises at a work retreat— I wasn't the type to let another person catch me. But I knew that I would only get the maximum effect if I let go. I took the deepest breath I could.

'If you take each step in the breathwork process as I lead you, the potential for the production of DMT is increased. It can provide or enhance spiritual insights and is associated with the highest states of meditation,' said Sam. 'DMT is traditionally thought to facilitate the soul's movement in and out of the body and is an integral part of birth and death experiences. It may also play an integral role in REM sleep and dreaming, and facilitate our connection to the universal human consciousness.' My curiosity was piqued.

Sam continued the process. Over and over again he said, 'Fully in . . . let it go.' Time became irrelevant. That in itself was a gift.

After several rounds—I couldn't even find the mind to count—I felt a shift in my body. I started to shake, and with each breath it became a stronger and stronger sensation. I wondered if this was happening to anyone else—surely this was strange?—but with Sam's advice still in my ears, I chose again to let myself go.

Okay, Sarah, you can do this, I thought to myself. *Let your body shake.*

And I did.

With this 'permission' I felt my body start to shake even more uncontrollably. I allowed it to do what it needed to do, and all the while Sam's gentle instructions filtered into my mind. He had led us into a new way of breathing—quick bursts of breath followed by extended breath holding—and it was working through me, increasing my autonomic regulation and sympathetic tone. This is when the muscle of the heart functions at peak efficiency as it circulates blood, and the nervous system has command of its fight-or-flight mechanism. I learnt later that uncontrollable shaking is a completely normal reaction. The process lasted an hour, even though it felt like it had only been minutes.

For the last out breath, Sam told us to roll our eyes back into our heads as if we were looking up and behind ourselves, with our eyelids closed. This would stimulate the natural production of DMT and help us enter a deep state of meditation. I felt someone caress my forehead in a loving way after I had closed my eyes, and to this day I am unsure if it was Sam or something else.

Then I felt a rush come over my body. It felt warm and benevolent, and I let myself fall deeply into the sensation. I felt a presence above me—a feeling that was real and very beautiful, even though I didn't have words to explain it. It just felt soft and unmistakable. It affected me so much I started to cry. At first just a few tears, and then my feelings were so heightened it turned to beautiful cleansing sobs. And in that space, I knew exactly who was there. I knew who this presence was. It was my friend Charlie, a beautiful man who I had shared many moments of joy and connection with when he was alive. A year earlier, Charlie had died by suicide. I had been devastated by the news and was still grieving his loss. Charlie was one of the most loving, intelligent, funny, charismatic people I had ever met. The giant hole he left behind would never be filled, and it was an ache that was palpable. And then, he was there above me. I could feel him.

I started talking to Charlie in my head.

'How are you, my darling friend?' I asked him. I could hear his reply with a clarity that filled me with awe.

'It's good to see you. I see you've been doing some amazing things,' he said. He still sounded just like Charlie. He'd always been full of interesting observations.

'I can't even find the words to tell you how much I miss you,' I said.

'Yeah, miss you too, lovely one,' he replied.

And so we went back and forth in a conversation that felt as real as when he was alive and would appear by my side asking me to go and get coffee with him.

The power of your breath

When you have these mystical moments in your life, you can't really question them. You alone know how real they are, and that is enough. I felt the truth of Charlie's presence in my bones. As we talked, I sobbed aloud—not because I was sad, but because I was filled with so much love. I missed him so much.

As the process drew to an end, a cellist started playing to call us back into the room and our ordinary state. I looked around me at the 30-plus people—most were strangers to me—who had also travelled this process. The majority of us were in tears. We sat together in a circle and each person took their turn to talk, if they wished, about their experiences. Many shared stories of visitations from loved ones, of profound messages of hope and encouragement, of insights into healing they could do for themselves or others. We had shared a collective experience despite our differences in age and vocation, every one of us from the tradies to the senior executives to the stay-at-home parents.

One beautiful lady—a grandmother living with Parkinson's—shared that she had received the message that her mind knew what to do to heal her body. She'd heard the message so clearly that she felt immediate relief and new hope for her health. She had a sense of peace about her that radiated from the inside, and she told us about the plans she was making to spend more time with her grandchildren. A young couple dealing with the heartbreak of the loss of a child had cradled each other as they shed tears together, along with reminders of happier times.

They honoured their little one by sharing stories about her with the group, finally able to move into acceptance and celebrate her short life. A man who had been hardened by terrible images that haunted him from his time in the armed services was on his knees as he accepted the caring embrace of newfound friends in the room. He later shared he had been so moved it had helped him to soften his heart and let go of hatred he had been carrying for two decades. A light had gone on inside him and he had been guided back to his ability to love. It was humbling to see and hear these profound changes. For everyone, the breathwork experience had been one of elevation and discovering new resources.

I was overwhelmed by the feeling of love—a natural high—and as the afternoon drew to a close, I hugged my friend Endi tightly. All I could say was, 'I am so grateful for you. Thank you so much for bringing me here.' Words could not adequately convey all the love I felt—love for my friend, love for the strangers who surrounded me, love for my teacher Sam, love for being alive. And, most of all, love for my new relationship with my breath, which had introduced me to a whole new field of possibilities.

•

Have you ever thought about how often you breathe, or what slow breathing might look like for you? The typical human respiratory rate is within the range of ten to twenty breaths per minute.

In some research, slow breathing is defined as four to ten breaths per minute.

Here's a little experiment. Set a timer for one minute and see what ten breaths a minute feels like. Then, try three seconds for your in breath, and three seconds for your out breath. We often take shallow breaths and only utilise the top part of our lungs. Now, try to breathe deep into the fullness of your chest cavity— or, even better, breathe deep into your abdominal cavity. Fill your lungs with fresh air. How does it feel in your body after one minute? Imagine how it would change your experience to breathe deep and slow more often, more readily, more consciously? This is the potential of your breath.

There are many breathing patterns you can experiment with, and many have specific benefits. Breathing practices such as the two-to-one breath cycle—breathing out for twice as long as you breathe in—help to regulate the motion of the lungs and quieten the nervous system.[15] It's useful for meditation (and the basis for alternate nostril breathing in the yogic tradition) but it also helps us prepare our body for physical exertion, so it can be beneficial before and during exercise. Many professional sportspeople use this technique, or variations of it, to enhance performance.

Breathing is directly connected to our autonomic nervous system. Stimulation of the nervous system happens with each inhalation and exhalation we take.[16] Our nervous system consists of the sympathetic nervous system and the parasympathetic nervous system. Both systems are stimulated without our conscious awareness and have different effects on the body. The sympathetic system helps the body gear up for things such as physical exercise or exertion; it increases our heart rate, muscle activity, blood pressure and sweat. The parasympathetic system prepares the body for rest, sleep or digestion and decreases the heart rate and so on. We can modulate these two systems in ways that benefit us through our breath. Inhalation is a sympathetic activity, while exhalation is a parasympathetic activity.

While breathing occurs without our conscious awareness, we can use it to our advantage via deliberate practices and different breathwork techniques. My experience at the retreat was one type of breathwork that influenced my nervous system and expanded my energy system. We can explore new capacities within our being and expand our minds with the breath—with the intention of gathering new tools and enhancing our lives. It's really useful to have a teacher or guide in this space, so I encourage you to seek out people and resources that help you find your own potential.

Another breathing pattern you will come across is called humming bee breathing. This fun technique involves breathing combined with a humming sound, so find a place where you feel free to make as much noise as you need to. Once you are seated and ready, place your first fingers over the little half-moon-shaped cartilage at the opening to your ear canal. Take a generous breath in and gently press your fingers into the cartilage as you exhale. As you exhale, make a loud humming sound, keeping your mouth closed. Hum for as long as you find comfortable and then repeat. This deep rhythmic breathing pattern may be useful to reduce anxiety, promote instant calm and help you fall asleep more readily. It can reduce stress levels and has other health benefits that create an overall feeling of wellbeing.

It is also well understood that cortisol (stress hormone) levels can be reduced through breathing, especially deep breathing into the pelvis where the vagus nerve—the main nerve of the parasympathetic nervous system—is located.

•

When I interviewed psychologist and world meditation leader Tara Brach for *A Life of Greatness*, I was taken by her perspective on breath and meditation. She told me that there is 'euphoria between our thoughts'. I believe what she meant was that, as we slow the breath and create open and clear space between the inhale and the exhale, there is a beauty that is ever-present and accessible. She likens this to a natural state where we can accept the reality of the moment and see the gold in who we are. The real blessing is that when we do this for ourselves, we see it more in others.

Tara said the essence of breathing is to give and receive—the breath is an endless cycle of exchange between ourselves and the world around us. The breath is a unifying factor that brings us into harmony with nature and each other. Slowing the breath lets us pause and accept where we are at any given moment, to quieten and see the joy. Breath is a way we can give love back to ourselves. Breathe into parts of the body that need your attention or healing and feel what happens. Breathe life-giving love into your cells, your veins and your organs. Breath is self-care. Breath becomes an act of radical acceptance.

Conscious breathing brings something additional to your meditation practice and helps you to take the idea of 'active' meditation a step further. Breathwork has been the key for me to go deeper and experience more. I have now learnt many different breathing techniques, some with sound releases and patterns that help raise my energy.

When you are faced with a stressful situation or trying to recover from one, a breathing technique can be an effective way to support the body and mind. This is why these methods are often taught to people in high-stress occupations. Keep in mind that it's counterproductive to feel stressed about getting the breathing right, so relax with it and let it happen. Make sure you are sitting or lying down when you first start to practise. Feeling lightheaded is common and a sign you are doing it right. If it's uncomfortable to begin with, try reducing the time you are counting. What is most important is that you are feeling a relaxation response, not that you are doing it as per the 'rules'. Everyone is different.

Creating a short five-minute window every day during which you practise conscious breathwork can be a great reset. You can also try to improve the way you breathe, specifically in through the nose and out through the mouth, so that your unconscious breaths are deeper, more even and more nourishing every moment of every day. It doesn't have to be difficult, just consistent and done with loving kindness. Through understanding and harnessing our breath, we can reach a greater sense of fulfilment in our lives and foster a deeper understanding of ourselves— essential to creating a life of greatness.

Without the breath we would not survive. With the breath, especially the conscious breath, we can be truly alive.

Chapter 15

Coming home

What lies behind us and what lies before us are tiny matters compared to what lies within us.

Henry Stanley Haskins

Every day we make hundreds of decisions about the life we want to live. Every time we choose to do one thing over another, every thought we allow to direct our choices, every moment we act on our impulses, we are directing the course of our life. We make small decisions that when added together become our life plans, whether we are aware of this or not. Our ability to stop, feel into and hold space for conscious choices is a skill that is within our power to master, and it is life-changing. We can't move forward into our life of greatness—we can't become self-actualised—without first developing this consciousness. We can't make the changes we seek without first being aware of where we are, what we are doing and why.

From this moment on, I invite you to notice what you think about. I invite you to create space between your thoughts and how you then respond or act. I invite you to observe how you express yourself. What words do you choose to describe your day? What words come naturally to you when you greet another person? When you have conversations with loved ones, what beauty do you bring to their lives, and therefore your own? I invite you to hear how you talk to yourself. Do you bring loving kindness to the internal chatter that exists in your own head? Do you hold yourself in a warm embrace and speak with truth and care to yourself? The words you choose mark your way of being. It is a simple and powerful truth that we create our reality every single day depending on how we speak to ourselves.

When you notice these tendencies in yourself, you can then shift the needle. You can start making real changes. What you notice you can change, but it is impossible to take a single step towards a life of greatness without first becoming aware of what is going on inside your mind. If you don't do the work to develop this awareness, this book will become another relic on your shelf of good intentions. So start, in this moment, by bringing your attention to what you are doing and what you are saying. Notice your actions, even the smallest ones. Notice what makes you sad, angry, happy or full of joy. Acknowledge the goodness in what you observe. Where you can't see value, commit to transform- ing those thoughts and actions into something better, something more aligned with the person you know you are becoming. It takes dedication and steadfastness to build the skill of awareness, but you can start right now and it will get easier as you practise.

The reality is that no change can happen without you first showing up. Sometimes you may even feel you are reaching the edge of your comfort zone; that is a good thing. Push yourself. Take a leap into the unknown. Growth can only occur when you explore the boundaries. You will be surprised at your capacity to change, and you will marvel at how quickly incremental steps can gain incredible momentum—but you have to put in the work. You have to not only decide you want change, but also live that change for the rest of your life.

These days, I live by this little snippet of wisdom: 'Move closer to the things that bring you joy.' It is in moments of joy that you will experience the homecoming your soul seeks. You will come home to a place inside yourself that only you have the power to reach. No one else can do it for you. You can look for all kinds of external supports and stimulus in your attempt to find our joy or discover your true self, but the simple truth is that all you seek is already part of who you are. Inside of you is the greatest version of yourself just waiting to be seen and reanimated.

Pause for a moment and imagine who you are without limits. This is the beauty that is ready to burst through and shape your life forever. Imagine coming home to this place inside you now. Bring it to life—bring it to *your* life.

Life will have more meaning. Everything you do will carry greater significance. Your life will have more of everything. It will be dynamic, tender, exciting and infinitely more fruitful. I can tell you this because this is how living with consciousness and seeking joy has shifted my own life towards one of greatness.

·

There is one question that people ask me almost without fail after I have given a talk: 'Do you ever have a bad day?' People want to know if I ever feel upset or angry. They want to know if things ever go wrong for me. I think they expect me to have some magical answer or piece of advice that might help them avoid unpleasant situations forever. But there is no such thing. I can only answer in truth and confirm that, yes, of course I have hard things happen: challenging times, angry moments. But what I have found since doing this work—since adopting all of the practices that I have talked about in this book—is that when things inevitably go pear-shaped I can bounce back so much more quickly. The ability to restore my heart and my being to a place of balance is much more available to me. I have resilience. This means I am able to regain my centre with greater ease and speed. I embrace choice, and this enhances my personal power. I see the challenges of life as speedbumps. You can't entirely avoid them, but you can notice them for what they are and respond to them with clarity and consciousness. You can retain a feeling of buoyancy regardless of what is going on, and move through life's challenges with grace and self-compassion. This will lead you into greater joy and a deeper sense of contentment.

No human is devoid of negative emotions. We are all going to feel a range of emotions, positive and negative, if we are fully alive. We can learn to transform our negative emotions into something more life-enhancing. We expend so much energy trying to avoid our negative emotions. Imagine if we could channel this energy into greater beauty in our lives? Imagine just allowing those emotions, all of them, to be—to notice them without becoming them.

Emotions are not exclusive. We can feel many emotions at once. We can learn how to hold all these feelings and understand we don't need to exclude or prioritise any. Mindfulness helps us understand and respond to our emotions in ways that deepen our sense of agency and happiness. We can be feeling deep sadness yet find pockets of happiness in our day, and that's okay. We can find dark humour in our challenges or sit in a feeling of radiant love, yet also be heartbroken that we are distant from a beloved.

This is how you move closer to the greatness within you. It doesn't matter who you are; these tools allow you to respond to your life from a place that can hold the complexity of being human. Without avoidance and distractions, you can be yourself, and live more deeply in authenticity and greatness.

When you do you, you affect a shift at every level of your life. It will be especially transformative in your relationships. What does it mean to be you? What do you hold sacred in your connections with others? A simple law of nature is that we get back what we give out, and this alone can create a sense of homecoming in your life. When you are living authentically, the people around you will notice—whether consciously or unconsciously. This can help them on their journey, too. Your ability to change your life, to live greatly, will be a leading light. People will see you. You can't change other people, but you can illuminate a pathway for them. Your example of change can guide others. This is how you build your community of people.

It is compelling to see others living in their full capacity, in their gloriousness. I find myself drawn to those who are living authentically, aligned with their purpose. Purpose brings meaning to our lives and leads us directly towards greatness. I don't think it's a coincidence that the people who live in this way might also be described as living a life of service. Whenever I ask my podcast guests 'What is a life of greatness?' the most-often-repeated response is 'Living in service to others'. Being in service comes with the capacity to live consciously. The two are knitted together as a way of life that brings meaning not only to you, but everyone around you. Our need to contribute to something greater than ourselves is how we create a better world together. I find this the most humbling yet animating reason for why we might strive to be the very best version of ourselves. It is never just all about us.

With greatness comes great freedom. In our search for what makes us happy, what brings us joy and a sense of belonging, we are released from the expectations of what we should have, or should be. This is a personal freedom that we experience deep in our core. The ability to unlock ourselves from others' expectations and societal demands that don't serve us is an act of freedom that lets us be happy in our own truth, comfortable in our own skin. That ever-present sense of lack, of needing something new, disappears as if by magic and we can appreciate what we already have. We become more content with our lives. We don't need to worry about the same things we used to find consuming. The stuff we thought was important fades into the background as we acquire something much more profound and life-changing: ourselves. We are softened by this freedom. We are allowed to exist just as we are, and we can afford this same freedom to others in our life. Of course, we don't accept bad behaviour from others; but we find a release in acceptance and love when we allow expectations to fall away. We find that our needs will be taken care of, and a sense of abundance may prevail. Monetary value is replaced by a deeper sense of worth, and we gain the ability to cope no matter what. We believe in different things, and we believe in ourselves.

Your greatness is not something that can be measured against others. It's important to arrive at your own personal interpretation of what greatness looks like for you, and hold yourself accountable against that understanding. Create a list of your values to keep you steady. Some commonly expressed core values include integrity, adaptability, discipline, uniqueness, assertiveness, open-mindedness, personal growth, flexibility, wellness, family, self-respect, altruism, dependability, generosity and courage, but there are dozens of options. Some of these words may resonate with you. Gather like words into clusters and look for overarching themes and connections. Relate these words to your own life, to who you are and who you seek to be. These values are your blueprint, a set of guiding principles to living authentically. Your experiments, your mistakes and your learnings are also part of this blueprint.

These new ways of thinking can be challenging to integrate. They might feel like a rebellion against societal norms and the way you were brought up to think and behave. Risk being seen as nonconforming if this means taking a stand for what you believe in, regardless of what others think. My suggestion is to be curious. Scrutinise any values or 'inherited' ideas in your life that feel off. Dare to question yourself and your beliefs. Audit your thoughts. Invest in your own growth daily. Educate yourself in other ways of thinking and expand your capacity to see different points of view. Somewhere in all of that is your own unique way of being.

Pick up what serves, put down what doesn't. It's completely up to you to create the life and belief system that lets you truly shine in your own greatness. No one else will have all the answers; those answers are inside you. You get to undertake the most incredible journey of self-discovery to find them.

I don't for a minute suggest this is easy, but it will get easier as you go along. Like anything worth doing you will need to find courage to stand in your own truth. You will need to persist, sometimes in the face of disappointment or others' questions. You will need to be determined, and know your own values intimately. You will find yourself feeling alone at times, and that is okay. It is sometimes necessary to have solitude in this process, but you are also building a new home for yourself that attracts like-minded souls who add to your sense of peace and joy. Slow and steady is the key. If you have come this far you have already shown you have the will and the personal drive to keep going. This is a lifetime practice. You may feel you will never quite arrive, but I can assure you the journey gets better and better along the way. What you achieve can never be taken from you. Following your dreams is your birthright.

With your eyes open, as you look at the world with a newfound awareness, you will realise there are people all around you who you can look to for guidance and inspiration. There are people right now waiting to shine your greatness back to you. Seek them out. The wise man who gets chatting to you at the local coffee shop while you wait for your latte, the workshop attendee who shares a story that transforms your understanding of healing—open your heart to the stories, fables and anecdotes being shared all around you. Read inspiring stories about people you admire, people who may illuminate a path for you. Look to the elders, the historians, the radicals and the helpers. There are people who have walked their own paths and who may guide your own steps. You can't be what you can't see.

It's funny how often we search for something far and wide, only to realise what we truly need has been right there within us all along. In *The Wizard of Oz*, Dorothy embarks on an incredible journey to the Emerald City to seek the all-powerful wizard to help her find her way home. We know this story deep in our bones. Along the way, she encounters companions who all believe they lack something—the Scarecrow in search of a brain, the Tin Man seeking a heart and the Lion who wants to find courage. But as they face challenges together, they come to realise these qualities were never truly missing. I think that's how it is as we search for our own greatness. We often think we need external validation or some magical fix to fulfil our dreams, yet the reality is that the strength, wisdom and passion we seek are already woven into the very fabric of our being.

Dorothy discovers her ruby slippers had the power to take her home from the very beginning. We too have an innate capability to navigate our own Yellow Brick Road called life. As we uncover our own greatness, we realise it is not about finding a wizard out in the world; it's about recognising and harnessing the magic that resides within us—perhaps with a little sprinkle of guidance from someone who has travelled a similar road.

As you have journeyed through this book, I hope you have also found the truth of your own becoming. Returning to the truth of who you are is not just a story for the big screen—it is the epic masterplan of your life. Coming home is the journey you set out on the day you were born, and it truly makes no sense at all to waste another moment of your precious life wondering about what might be. Harness your greatness knowing that you are not alone. Be the authentic person that you are, and bring your brightness to the world at a time when it is absolutely necessary that we all shine. Start now with the simple decision to take a step. While it is a personal journey, it is a grand story and one we all share. I have walked my own road and I will always be on this path.

Wherever you have been and whatever you have been doing, a fulfilling life of greatness is now in front of you. It's time to take the first step and embrace your full potential. Around you, the world is already rising up to support you in all you seek. And beside you, the right people are appearing.

We are all capable of greatness.

You have what you need to find your way home.

References

1   Stanford University, 2012, 'According to Prof. Luskin, we have over 60,000 thoughts a day with 90% being repetitive', X, <https://twitter.com/Stanford/status/188027203383066624>, accessed 5 June 2024.

2   K. Cherry, 2023, 'What is the negativity bias?', *Verywell Mind*, <www.verywellmind.com/negative-bias-4589618>, accessed 5 June 2024.

3   D. Henley, 2021, 'Master this skill to connect more effectively with your team', *Forbes*, <www.forbes.com/sites/dedehenley/2021/08/29/master-this-skill-to-connect-more-effectively-with-your-team/>, accessed 6 June 2024.

4   C.R. Rogers & F.J. Roethlisberger, 1991, 'Barriers and gateways to communication', *Harvard Business Review*, <https://hbr.org/1991/11/barriers-and-gateways-to-communication>, accessed 6 June 2024.

5   D.R. Hamilton, *Five Side Effects of Kindness: This book will make you feel better, be happier & live longer*, UK: Hay House, 2021.

6   R.D. Lane, 'Neural correlates of conscious emotional experience', in R.D. Lane & L. Nadel (eds), *Cognitive Neuroscience of Emotion*, New York: Oxford University Press, 2000, pp. 345–370.

7   S. Allen, S 2018, 'The science of gratitude', Greater Good Science Center, <https://ggsc.berkeley.edu/images/uploads/GGSC-JTF_White_Paper-Gratitude-FINAL.pdf>, accessed 14 June 2024.

8   S. Allen, 'The science of gratitude'.

9   L. Toussaint, E. Worthington & D.R. Williams, *Forgiveness and Health: Scientific evidence and theories relating forgiveness to better health*, Springer, 2015.

10 S. Schnall et al., 'Social support and the perception of geographical slant', *Journal of Experimental Social Psychology*, 2008, vol. 44, no. 5, pp. 1246–1255.

11 S. Allen, 2022, 'How biology prepares us for love and connection', *Greater Good Magazine*, <https://greatergood.berkeley.edu/article/item/how_biology_prepares_us_for_love_and_connection>, accessed 15 June 2024.

12 J. Holt-Lunstad, T.B. Smith & J.B. Layton, 'Social relationships and mortality risk: A meta-analytic review', *PLoS Medicine*, 2010, vol. 7, no. 7.

13 E.S. Kim et al., 'United we thrive: friendship and subsequent physical, behavioural and psychosocial health in older adults (an outcome-wide longitudinal approach)', *Epidemiology and Psychiatric Sciences*, 2023, vol. 32, no. 65.

14 A. Kotifani, 2018, 'Moai—This tradition is why Okinawan people live longer, better', *Blue Zones*, <www.bluezones.com/2018/08/moai-this-tradition-is-why-okinawan-people-live-longer-better>, accessed 15 June 2024.

15 J. Clarke, n.d., 'Soothe your nervous system with 2-to-1 breathing', *Yoga International*, <https://yogainternational.com/article/view/soothe-your-nervous-system-with-2-to-1-breathing>, accessed 16 June 2024.

16 M. Rubin, 2020, 'Brain, spinal cord, and nerve disorders', *MSD Manual Consumer Version*, <www.msdmanuals.com/en-au/home>, accessed 16 June 2024.

Resources

L isten to Sarah on her top-rated podcast, *A Life of Greatness*, where she and her guests share their research, knowledge and experiences to help you cultivate an extraordinary existence. In these conversations and talks you'll learn the simple tips, habits, practices and strategies to help you unlock your best self and future, starting now. Available at www.sarahgrynberg.com/podcast, Apple Podcasts and Spotify.

Podcast episodes referenced in this book

Sarah Blondin: How to get out of your head and into your heart

Tara Brach: Loving what is

Bruce Bryan: Wrongfully imprisoned for nineteen years

Dr David Hamilton: The power of placebo and the five side effects of kindness

Dr Richard Harris: Why risk taking can bring you extraordinary success

Jack Kornfield: The end of suffering

Scarlett Lewis: Choosing compassion and forgiveness

Matthew McConaughey: How to live your best life

Anand Mehrotra: The secrets to a happy life

Dan Millman: Living with a peaceful heart and warrior spirit

Carolyn Myss: Living in the light

Marissa Peer: Transforming your life

Bruce Perry: You are more than your story

Yung Pueblo: The journey of self-love

Sharon Salzberg: Finding your way back to joy

Dr Richard Schwartz: The therapy that is changing people's lives

Robin Sharma: Your everyday hero

Dr Julie Smith: A practical toolkit for better mental health

Bronnie Ware: The five regrets of the dying

David Whyte: Heal your pain

Gary Zukav: Creating authentic power

Acknowledgements

It has been a pleasure to create this book for my *A Life of Greatness* community and all those who open its cover. I feel blessed to have this opportunity to reach into your world and share this wisdom with you.

To my mum and dad, who are always full of love. Thank you for your never-ending support and your faith in me. I love you both dearly. You fostered in me the ability to dream and gave me all I needed to turn my dreams into reality. This has helped me get where I am today, and I am incredibly grateful. My mum was one of my very first listeners and has never missed an episode of my podcast.

I'd like to acknowledge my grandmother, Susie, one of the kindest people I am blessed to know. You taught me how to be strong and are the epitome of resilience. Your happy disposition is infectious. I love being around you.

To my beautiful family, I want to say thank you for being part of my world. To my caring son Oliver, you are wise beyond your years, and you have always expressed how proud you are of me. You're my biggest fan and I truly appreciate you reading chapters of the book and offering your sound advice.

To my daughter Poppy, you are forever supportive and loving, and have such a zest for life. I love that you believe the sky is the limit and live with a heart full of big dreams. I will always be here to help you move towards them. Being in your world allows me to dream large, too.

To my husband, you are my greatest companion and friend, and I'm grateful for your unwavering support. You've spent time reading this book and providing me with honest and smart advice, and I appreciate your deep wisdom. You are an incredible sounding board and provide me with the best 'unbiased' feedback.

Many years ago, I was given the opportunity of a lifetime because Grant Tothill at Southern Cross Austereo believed in me. Thank you for seeing me and allowing me to shine. You helped bring the first episode of the *A Life of Greatness* podcast to the world, and you supported me as I made the transition from radio producing. Thanks to you for your continued mentorship. And to Dave Cameron for moving me into the podcast team all those years ago.

Thank you also to John Kelly from Southern Cross Austereo. You have always championed me and have given me valuable feedback on more episodes of *A Life of Greatness* than I can count.

Acknowledgements

You understood instinctively how my podcast could change lives and help people on their journey.

I extend my heartfelt gratitude to Hamish Blake and Andy Lee. As your executive producer over four remarkable years, your unwavering kindness and care were truly inspiring. Your success is a testament to your characters, leading with a generosity of spirit. The wisdom gained and the laughter shared while working on your show have been invaluable.

To all of my *A Life of Greatness* podcast listeners. If it wasn't for you, this book may never have come to be. You put a precious idea in my head, and I am proud to share this book with you now as a testament to your encouragement and loyalty.

To all the incredible studio guests who have featured on *A Life of Greatness*. You have shared with candidness, wisdom and generosity. Many of you have become my biggest champions, even flying the flag internationally for me. I am so glad that we are able to co-create inspiring content together.

My gratitude to all the people who have shared stories with me over the years, and particularly to those who have been so generous in contributing their stories to this book. I have changed names and some details to protect privacy, so I am not able to name you all, but be assured my heart is full of respect and love for you.

I am also fortunate to have a network of deep and committed friendships in my life—people who have shaped who I am and supported me with unending loyalty and a safe haven to land. I appreciate your calls, our times of laughter and your shoulders to cry on. You're always there for me, and I will always be there for you.

To the editorial team at Allen & Unwin, Tessa, Sally, Greer and Brooke. Thank you for holding my hand throughout this process. A first book is a huge undertaking and your guidance, feedback and wise words are truly appreciated as we have shaped this text. It has been a pleasure to work with you.

My beautiful dog Lola. You were my steady companion as I wrote these words, gently snoring at my feet. Special pats for you always.

Books can only happen with the love, guidance and support of many people and it's impossible to mention everyone. I am grateful to you all and wish you all a fulfilled existence.